SOME LIVING MASTERS
OF THE PULPIT

JOSEPH FORT NEWTON

SOME LIVING MASTERS OF THE PULPIT

Studies in Religious Personality

BY

JOSEPH FORT NEWTON

Essay Index Reprint Series

 BOOKS FOR LIBRARIES PRESS
FREEPORT, NEW YORK

INTERNATIONAL STANDARD BOOK NUMBER:
0-8369-2287-5

LIBRARY OF CONGRESS CATALOG CARD NUMBER:
71-152203

PRINTED IN THE UNITED STATES OF AMERICA

TO

CHARLES CLAYTON MORRISON

LEADER AND COMRADE
IN THE SERVICE OF A GREATER CHRISTIANITY

WITH ADMIRATION, GRATITUDE AND
PERSONAL AFFECTION

INVOCATION

With curious regularity every age has bewailed the passing of the pulpit; but the great office abides—persistent, permanent, precious—surviving new theories of knowledge and old conditions of life, helped, not hurt, by the skyline being set back. When Mahaffy wrote "The Decay of Modern Preaching" in 1882, Parker, Liddon, Spurgeon, Maclaren, Beecher, Brooks, Broadus and Simpson were in the full splendour of their powers! It must be that men do not see what is passing before their eyes, because they are so busy weaving a robe of romance for the past. The chorus of complaint has been unusually loud in our time, as witness these words which suggested the following sketches:

"If the great sermons which contain the philosophy of Bishop Butler were preached today, would they fill the smallest church in London? For the present, at least, the noble art of the pulpit must be considered as lost.

There exists for it neither favorable conditions, nor the indispensable audience, nor
apparently even the artists themselves.   It
awaits, like so many other of the arts—like
great painting, like great poetry—the return
of the mind of Europe to an assured and all-
pervading religious faith."

Thus even the London *Times* joins in the
litany of lament that the pulpit of today is in
eclipse, forgetting that if preaching depended
on a willing response to prophetic voices it
would have ceased long since.   Of course the
sermons of Bishop Butler would not fill even
a small London church today—the times have
changed, the taste is different—and one recalls
how in his own day the Bishop sat in his castle
brooding over the decay of religion, while the
miners, touched by the wondrous evangelism
of Wesley, were singing hymns of praise almost under his window.   Surely we have not
yet realised the full import of those words of
Jesus which echo like a refrain through the
Gospels, "He that hath ears to hear, let him
hear."

Hence a series of studies of some living
masters of the pulpit—impressionistic and im-

perfect enough, and selecting only a few out of
many shining examples—intended to show that
the divine art of preaching is not lost, and in
the hope that elect young men may be won to
its high service. Indeed, my task has been
made difficult not by the barrenness of the
modern pulpit, but by the richness, variety and
comprehensiveness of its Christian witness in
a tangled time. Grateful to God for many
others of equal genius and charm, if I have
written of preachers of whom I have vivid
and moving memories, it is because such experiences enable one to write with more insight
and understanding—and, perhaps, to repro-
duce somewhat of the atmosphere and impress
of personality.

Anybody can find fault, but some of us have
learned to give thanks for what men can do,
rejoicing in their gifts without dwelling on
their limitations. Goethe has a golden sentence
in which he tells how, as he grew older, the
beautiful feeling entered his mind that only
mankind together is the true man, and that
the individual can only be happy when he has
the courage to feel himself in the whole. It is
so in our Christian ministry, if we have the

grace to know our brethren, and especially
those who can do what we cannot do, making
their work our own by appreciation. No two
men could be more unlike than Dean Inge and
Bishop Quayle—no two farther apart in point
of view than Dr. Truett and Dr. Crothers—
but all of them are our brethren, and together
they make a goodly, gracious company in whose
many keys and cadences the Everlasting Gospel
is made eloquent.

Such a study suggests many reflections, one
of which is that if we are to have Christian
Unity it must be by virtue of the insight which
divines one Spirit, one purpose, one passion
underlying differing gifts and points of view.
Here are trinitarians, unitarians, radicals,
conservatives, liberals, evangelicals—scholars,
orators, pastors, teachers, evangelists, a noble
layman and a great woman—yet the tie that
binds them into a radiant fellowship is a devout
life devoted to the service of a common Master
whose they are, and whose Gospel they preach
each with his own accent and emphasis. At last,
or soon or late, the truth as it is in Jesus, res-
cued from the sectarianism which has obscured
it, will rise and shine by its own splendour

—profounder than all philosophies, yet as simple as the prayer of a child—revealing its reality as a Life not a system, a Person not a dogma, and finding its fulfilment in a Beloved Community.

Some one ought to follow these sketches with a series of studies of the New Preaching now developing, at once so direct in method and so full of promise, and which seeks to interpret the Gospel in its relation to the new issues, new outlooks, and new enterprises which preoccupy the thought of men in our time. Since the Great War a new note has been heard in our Christian message, a new emphasis and implication—differing from the old as Salvation differs from Salvage—and there is a gallant company of young men in all communions to whom it is the Word of God for our age. It is for us to preach "the Gospel of the Kingdom" with veracity of mind and humility of heart, speaking the truth in the spirit of Jesus, remembering the exhortation of St. Vincent:

"O priest, O expositor, O doctor, if the Divine gift hath made thee fit by genius, training and learning, be thou Bazaleel of the

spiritual tabernacle; engrave the precious gems
of Divine doctrine; faithfully fit them together; adorn them wisely; add splendor,
grace, loveliness. Let that which was formerly
believed darkly, be understood clearly by thy
exposition. Let posterity by thy aid rejoice in
truths understood, which antiquity venerated
without understanding them. Yet teach still
the same things which thou didst learn, so that
although thou speakest in a new fashion, thou
speakest not new things."

J. F. N.

Church of the Divine Paternity.
New York City.

CONTENTS

SOME LIVING MASTERS
OF THE PULPIT

SOME LIVING MASTERS
OF THE PULPIT

I: George A. Gordon

As one of a host of students who used to throng the galleries of the Old South Church—just as they do today—I confess that it is not easy for me to write about Dr. Gordon calmly. Under God I owe more to that gracious and wise preacher than to any living man, and but for his influence upon me—alike by the nobility of his character, the integrity of his intellect, and the richness of his insight—at a time when nothing was certain but uncertainty, I should not be in the pulpit today. God be thanked for the leadership of authentic teachers of faith in the critical, formative years of youth—next to good mothers they are the best gifts of God! It was a joy, as well as an honour, to stand in the pulpit of Old South Church and bear such testimony, both for myself and for a vast com-

pany of young men whom his ministry has
blessed, on the evening before I set sail to take
up my labours at the City Temple.

Others have written of Dr. Gordon as a
theologian, ranking him in the dynasty of Ed-
wards and Bushnell, as the third truly great
constructive theologian that America has
known.[1] With this estimate I am in full agree-
ment, and with the further verdict that in the
scope and quality of his labour as a Christian
thinker, no less than in the originality and fruitfulness of his total accomplishment—bringing
to the service of faith not only exact thinking
and ample learning, but a high and tender
humanity, an ennobling imagination, and the
transfiguring insight of a poet—he out-tops his
peers and stands alone. The House of Doctrine, needed for the comfort and habitation of
the intellect, and as a shelter for the holy things
of faith, is a temple ever "building and built
upon." As between the easy-going agnosticism,

[1] *Progressive Religious Thought in America*, by J. W.
Buckham, of the Pacific School of Religion, contains a chapter
entitled, "George A. Gordon: The New Theology Universal-
ized,"—though by New Theology he does not mean the movement associated with the City Temple. For an early conservative critique, see "Dr. G. A. Gordon's Reconstruction of
Christian Theology," by Dr. A. H. Plumb, *Bibliotheca Sacra*,
April, 1896. The article makes rather interesting reading today.

so widespread in the modern world—often
only a labour-saving device to escape the toil
of high thinking—and the artificial "block
universe" of the old dogmatic theology, Dr.
Gordon has been a wise master-builder in an
era of theological break-up, building once more
a House of Faith in the midst of the years.

It has been the fashion of late years to make
light of theology—forgetting that it is not
theology that is wrong, but wrong theology
that needs to be reinterpreted—and to all such
glib and superficial judgments the ministry of
Dr. Gordon has been a standing rebuke. Like
Plato, "the father of theology," he holds that
"an unexamined life is unlivable," and that
religion must be not simply a life of the spirit—
much less a series of chance thoughts and
vagrant insights—but an order of ideas, con-
trolling the issues of the heart through the
authority of its teaching over the mind. Else
it will be an empty emotion or a mere superstition. Hence his task and his toil, pursued
with single-hearted devotion, making his
labour a fulfilment of his own description of
the older New England divines, "the teacher
of the people, the former of their minds in

Christian belief, the thinker who covered their existence with the power of a consistent thought of the universe." At once critical and creative, his study of the old New England theology is a piece of analytic and synthetic criticism which it would be difficult to match in the entire literature of theology, showing how life acts upon abstractions as fresh air acts upon mummies—how they crumble to *dust* and blow away. But in its place he has helped to erect upon surer foundations a more spacious Home of the Soul, and we behold "the sweet heavens built in unity and dominion and power, and under them the obedient, awestruck, and yet hopeful world of men." Nor must we forget that Dr. Gordon, like the apostolic succession of great thinkers in which he stands, has toiled not as a technical theologian, but as a preacher in the active service of the church, living not in the half lights of a few arid and well-domesticated abstractions, but in the vision of truth as it stands in the service of our piteous, passionate, and pathetic human life.

No one questions that Dr. Gordon is a great preacher, but we learn very little from that fact, because great preachers are of many

kinds; chiefly of two kinds, as he himself once
pointed out in an exquisite tribute to Dr.
Munger. There is the type represented in
America by Beecher and Brooks, and in England by Parker and Spurgeon—"the fiery
orator, the master of assemblies, the cyclonic
commander of the assent and homage of the
multitude." Such a preacher is properly placed
in a great centre of population, where he may
make his audience by a process of gradual
selection from among the mass of those to
whom his individual quality appears; but it is
delusion fatal to the ministry to imagine that
there is no other type of great preacher. There
is the type represented by Bushnell and
Munger, by Martineau and Tipple—who
preached such sermons as Emerson might have
preached had he remained in the pulpit, and
whom Ruskin called "the greatest master of
pulpit prose." This preacher is no striking
orator. He can never be popular except with
a few select minds. He prevails mightily, but
it is by the depth and vitality of his ideas, by
the intensity and clarity of his vision of God,
and by the form and beauty which he presses
into the service of his vocation. He is the

scholar, the thinker, the seer, and his power lies wholly in his message and in his high concern to utter it. He influences men deeply, especially young men who are caught up into the radiance of his vision, and he remains a fertilising power long after he passes away. No one will deny that Bushnell is more than a peer of Beecher or Parker; at least our admiration for the orator must not blind us to the right of Munger and Martineau to an equal honour in the ministry.

More nearly than any man in our generation —more nearly than any preacher I can recall— Dr. Gordon has united these two types of preaching; the thinker and the orator, the scholar and the artist; the prophet and the man of letters; the theologian whose sermons are lyrics and whose theology is an epic. If he is not widely known as an orator, it is because his devotion to his high task has kept him too much from the great assemblies of the church; and he has not been at the beck and call of patriotic, social, and academic fraternities, with the result that there is no body of secular oratory by him, as there was in the case of Beecher. But at his best, in his great hours of

vision and conquest—especially when he drops
manuscript and lets himself go—Dr. Gordon
is an orator of incomparable power, of unique
and compelling charm, who can make smiles
and tears alternate as swiftly as Beecher did;
"whose touch is light enough for the after-
dinner speech, with its potpourri of wit and
story, yet commanding and weighty enough on
occasion to shape the policies of church and
state." Those who have not heard him when
he is deeply stirred, and dealing with a great
theme before an expectant throng, do not know
him at his highest and best. The sweep and
grasp and grandeur of his thought, aglow with
virility, sympathy, and abounding hope, and
shot through with the colour, fire and beauty
of a poet, is a thing of splendour. Master of a
picturesque, variegated and brilliant homiletic,
his eloquence blooms into literature, and if
poetry is of his essence, "the prophet-warrior
in him exorcises the table-serving priest."

Surely no one can ever forget a service in
Old South Church, where all classes of people
mingle in an air of democratic fellowship.
There the Back Bay matron worships with the
simply-dressed school teacher, and the railroad

president and the brakeman on his line are equally at home. Boston is a hive of student life, proof of which is seen in the rows of eager, intelligent faces in the galleries. The preacher arrests attention by his stalwart frame, his massive head, his shaggy brows, his piercing eyes, and by the simple dignity of his manner. Tall, broad-shouldered, finely formed, one can well believe that he did good work in the iron-foundry when he came, "a lad of pairts," from Aberdeenshire to make his future in America. The face and figure are worthy of the brush of a great painter of men. Rugged yet gentle, it is a face that one can study for a long time, reading in it the story of his struggle upward, his fearless facing of the issues of thought, and his fight for a larger faith; and there are lines where smiles fall asleep when they are weary. For all his learning, he is a man of the people, and as he prays one feels that he not only knows people, but loves them. The prayer is neither hortatory nor declamatory, but brooding, tender and far-ranging in its sympathy, mindful alike of the joys and sorrows of home and of the burdens of the man of state. He talks with a God whose love is equal to his power, and there are phrases that haunt the heart for years, as when he seeks "the consolation of moral self-respect," or death is described as "the last, ineffable, homeward sigh of the soul."

When the sermon begins the mood of the preacher alters—disciplined thought takes the place of worshipful passivity, and the truth of the day is seen against a long background of philosophy and a far horizon of faith. His gestures are vigorous rather than graceful, as befits the forthright sinewiness of his thought, and if certain mannerisms are disconcerting at first, they are atoned for by a Scotch burr which still clings to his accent. The symmetry of the sermon is a feat of homiletic genius, and as its great power gathers and grows one feels that the secret of the preacher is that he has what Wordsworth called "the first great gift, the vital soul." Positive without being dogmatic, he has no "art of subtle phrases that touch the edge of assertion and yet stops short of it." What loftiness and range of thought, expounding the sublimity and tenderness of Christian faith; what gorgeous colouring of imagination, rich and vivid in its tints; what

analyses of character, done with the stroke
of the etcher; what wealth of allusion to literature, science, philosophy, the poets with whom
he lives and the eager, troubled, aspiring life of
man. Here is a man whose interest ranges
from Aristotle to the records of champion
athletes, equally at home in St. Augustine and
Alice in Wonderland, to whom nothing human
is alien or without meaning. There are scenes
from nature in many moods, gusts of elemental
feeling, and epithets Carlylean in their withering blast. Sunlight alternates with shadow,
and the swift, terse summing up of an individual character or an historical epoch—sur-
passing Fairbairn in vividness—is followed by
lines from Robert Burns so apt that they seem
to have been written for the day. But he knows
just how far he can lead us at the moment—
how much strain feeling and attention can
stand without fatigue—and before we are
aware of it some flash of bright humour, never
far away, has relieved the tension, before he
takes us with him to the triumphant conclusion.
Often we have a glimpse of his early days and
then one hears a note of sweet-toned, melting
pathos, as of one who knows the beauty and

sorrow of life and the sadness of its long
farewells:

I remember well the last walk that I took in
my native land before I sailed for the Western
world more than forty years ago. It was on
one of the longest and brightest days in June.
I had said good-bye to dear friends and my
solitary path for ten miles lay through peaceful
and fruitful farms and over the ridge of a
mountain whose shapely summit had looked
down upon the coming and going of im-
memorial generations of men. Then followed
a long stretch of moor, barren, dismal, whose
heather would in three months bloom again and
fade like the hopes in the hearts of poor human
beings. As I struck the moor, the sun was
setting. The lonely path lay in the great transfiguring radiance. It became a path of beauty
and infinite tender suggestion; a heavenly
meaning seemed to beat in the boundless glow;
a sense of companionship, not understood then,
settled in the heart, delight took the place of
loneliness, and the journey that thus lay in the
path of the setting sun I could not wish to end.
More than forty years have come and gone
since then. Farewells have been spoken to
many friends for the last time on earth. The
journey has been through much of the beauty
of the world, and still the way has been over
hill and moor, crag and torrent. The pilgrimage has often seemed a type of the lonely

and sorrowful migration of men from the shadows of morning to the gloom of the evening. The happiest experiences have not deafened me to the still sad music of humanity; the evanescence of all things earthly has been a constant refrain in my spirit. Despair and utter heart-break would long ago have undone my days if nothing heavenly had been found to glorify and comfort and protect the precious burden of human love.

"The light that never was on sea or land" enfolds the way of every pilgrim. He is travelling in the glow that falls upon time from the Eternal; his path is in the transfiguring presence of the Infinite Love. . . .

> Who would stop, or fear to advance,
> Though home or shelter he had none,
> With such a sky to lead him on? [2]

The first volume of sermons by Dr. Gordon— as distinguished from his essays and lectures —was published in 1906, and its appearance was both a religious and a literary event. It is entitled *Through Man to God,* and deals not with the passing moods and modes of thought, but with the fundamental issues of faith. What is final? What is sovereign? Who is God? How shall we appear before God? Is the

[2] *Revelation and the Ideal.*

character of the Eternal accessible to Man?
And if so, how? Along what path shall we
approach that character? No serious-minded
man can read these discourses without being
enlarged and enriched by them, and to have
listened to them must have been one of the
great inspirations of a life-time. In stateliness
of thought, in scope and clarity of insight, in
nobility of sentiment, in strength and beauty
of diction, they match the greatest sermons in
Christian history. The technique of the
preacher is forgotten in the majesty of his
thought, all is so spontaneous, so natural, so
free. The short sentence prevails, but the
poetic imagery of the style is in the fibre, not
in the dress of the thought. It is a vision of
God through humanity at its highest, and if it
is humanity that interprets God, only God can
adequately interpret humanity. The universe
is seen in its vastness as unveiled by science,
but despite its seeming moral contradictions, it
is the native country of the human spirit, for
God is in it and love is its final law. The
preacher lives with great men, great epochs,
great events; the old philosophers are his
fellows, the prophets and the classic poets, and

one learns that it is the great truths that are the home-speaking truths. What is the great meaning of it all? is the ever-recurring thought refrain of a volume the cumulative impression of which is simply overwhelming. The last sermon, "God All in All," is a theodicy exalting, subduing, satisfying—a sermon more majestic, more fundamentally true and beautiful it is difficult to imagine.[3]

With the theology of Dr. Gordon I have not to do, except to say this his chief service has

[3] Other volumes appeared later, notably *Revelation and the Ideal* in 1913; the fruit of ten years of study and reflection with the intent of writing a book on the philosophy of Revelation. Alas, the book had to be abandoned, and instead of a treatise we have a series of visions, the central insight of which is that "Moral Idealism and Revelation are but the concave and the convex of the same figure,"—the Ideal being the East where, in each new age, the Eternal light breaks in upon our human world. The book asks two of the profoundest questions in the entire sphere of religious interest: Does the Eternal God speak to man? If so, how? What the unwritten treatise might have been we can only imagine; but this scroll of vision is one of the golden books to those who believe that "the ideal is the shadow of God in the mind of man;" its depth of insight only equalled by the richness and variety of its exposition.

Still another volume appeared in 1916, entitled *Aspects of the Infinite Mystery*—a rather forbidding title for the most intimate and revealing of his books—perhaps as much of a spiritual biography of the preacher as we are ever likely to get. It was first a series of mid-week talks, then a series of sermons at the request of the Church, which by resolution asked that they be published. Here is the ripe, mellow thought of a man who has reached the time of life when he has "something on hand infinitely more serious than the attempt to get votes from either the liberal or conservative camp." He writes with his eyes on reality, and as life draws toward

been the transformation of our thought of God
from the partialism of a sovereign to the universal saving grace of a Father; and he is one
of the few men who has had the courage to
follow that vision through to its inevitable conclusion. My purpose here is not with his
theology, but with the art and genius with
which he has preached a faith not won without
struggle—as we learn from a bit of revealing
autobiography in the second of his lectures on
the *Ultimate Conceptions of Faith*. It is
thought by some that Dr. Gordon preaches
philosophy more than theology, and theology
more than religion, but that is to err; though
his published works might leave such an impression. But in the ordinary course of his

evening he finds that "something has been found that is im-
perishable," a sobered, purified, residual faith, the issue of
the discipline of time upon a free mind; a faith which many
waters cannot quench.

In the Book of Memory he finds a symbol of his thought,
in the three ways of crossing a stream in his boyhood home
in Scotland. The bridge, the ferry, and the stepping-stones
now represent to him dogmatic belief, ecclesiasticism, and
insight. Any one can cross the river of the mystery of life
on the bridge of a creed. All who are satisfied with a boat
can find an ideal method in sitting still and not upsetting the
Catholic tradition; but those who put their souls to a test
must pick their way over with the spirit of adventure. In
this familiar, homely fashion he deals with the vital issues
of faith and life, with now a flash of humour, now a touch of
pathos, and always a sense of wonder and mystery not inconsistent with a confident and happy outlook.

ministry it is not so. Life is above philosophy, and he touches its practical problems with the same insight and power with which he expounds the faith by which it is lighted and led, preaching righteousness so full of ideal splendour as to overawe and win the heart, and so instinct with love as to stir the sluggish will. On public questions he can withhold his thunder-bolts, but if he speaks the spade is called a spade, as Plutarch said of one of his characters. He follows no fads, and is duped by no delusions, nor does he have any patience with clap-trap:

The cry for a revival of religion is natural; but the religion to be revived is not the right kind. . . . For this end professional revivalism with its organisations, its staff of reporters who make the figures suit the hopes of good men, the system of advertisements, the exclusion or suppression of all sound critical comment, the appeals to emotion and the use of means that have no visible connection with grace, is utterly inadequate. The world awaits the vision, the passion, the simplicity, and the stern truthfulness of the Hebrew prophet; it awaits the imperial breadth and moral energy of the Christian Apostle of the nations. . . . I have spoken of the few elect souls, men and women, in our churches who are worthy to stand among the best of the Christian ages. What about the mass of church people? Are they not as fond of the polluted book, the play with its appeal to sensual passion, as their pagan neighbors? . . . Do they not know every avenue of exclusiveness and pride, every black art of gossip, every twist and turn of the ropes of inhumanity, and do they not attend church and look for the coming of the kingdom of God? What kind of a revival will meet this case? Hysteria will not do, nor the devoutness of Lent, nor a turn at psychic healing, whether as patient or patron. What is demanded here is the axe laid at the root of the tree; the new heaven and the new earth, wherein dwelleth righteousness; the renunciation of the devil and all his works, and the profound and sincere appeal to the Eternal God.[4]

There speaks a man who is as prodigal in his brotherliness as he is pungent in his rebuke of sin, sham, and unreality; a man to know whom is a religion. If there is such a thing as Christian envy, not evil but honourable—a kind of joyous jealousy in the presence of great work greatly done—the ministry of Dr. Gordon, alike by its completeness, its consistent devotion to an "august opportunity," and its fruitfulness

[4] *Religion and Miracle.*

in practical service, would excite such an emotion. One cannot overestimate the worth, both in achievement and example, of his years of high, incessant work, full of the peace of great thoughts and the chastening force of pure motives, undisturbed by vulgar popularity. Lovable as a friend, wise as an adviser, inspiring as a teacher, beloved as a shepherd of souls, the nearer one comes to him the more just and stainless he seems to be. No great preacher has ever been more responsive to the gallant and chivalrous love of his younger brethren, all of whom will join me in applying to him these words of his own, written of one whom he loved and admired:

Above all else for this high grace, we, his brethren in the ministry, revere and love him. Under his influence we feel upon our hearts the peace of God, and we do not grudge him his great gifts, his distinguished success or his place in the reverent esteem of thousands. He has blessed us with the sense of the grace that comes only from our Lord Jesus Christ, the love that issues from God the Father, and the friendship that stands in the communion of the Holy Spirit. Long may his witness continue. Long may he live in his hospitable home, among his books and his friends, with his fruitful pen busy in the service of the kingdom of heaven. In his day may there be no failing light, and when the inevitable evening comes may its soft farewell fires be lost in the glorious peace of the eternal morning.

II: John A. Hutton

In a series of sketches of living preachers by
Hugh Sinclair, in 1912, Dr. Hutton was included, but he did not come off very well. As
minister of the wealthy Belhaven Church, Glasgow, he was described as "a well-placed man,"
meaning that he fitted a well-groomed congregation of aristocratic people whom other people
like to know. Nor was it difficult, the author
said, to imagine the type of minister who goes
with such a church. He must be a man of
ability, of course, and he must possess the modern equivalent of "soundness in the faith,"
with a distinct talent for finding a foothold in
Scripture for the uneasy mind of the age.
Public-spirited, within well-defined limits, he
must be, with the maximum of social tact and
the knack of genial acquaintanceship; "and one
can imagine a gift for opportune silence super-
latively useful." Balance, sanity, a realistic
mental habit, a turn for middle ways, and a

diplomatic personality, were named as the
characteristics of the minister of Belhaven:

He is shrewd, terse and stimulating, flings
out the kind of a challenge that is provocative
without being provoking, makes his hearers
feel that he respects their views even when he
is demolishing them, states his points seriously
but without over-stringency. He has a sure
eye for the practically effective, is master of
the art of putting things, gives us the kind of
truth we can understand; has a gift of recon-
noitre and grip which commands the respect of
the hard-headed business man. "Clever" is
undoubtedly a word that fairly applies to him—
the question remains, in what sense? Does it
sum him up, or is it merely the pinch of salt in
his dish of wisdom? Is it of the disconcerting
order that breeds instinctive suspicion, or does
it add practical confidence to moral trust? Is
is merely a flair of the things that "go down"
with people, or an instinct for the shortest way
to lift people up? It does not take long to make
up one's mind on that score.

It is, indeed, the touch of sympathy that
dominates all his preaching—the sympathy of
the man who may not himself be deeply
acquainted with grief and anguish, but whose
fine intuition outruns his experience as John
outran Peter long ago. To the problems which
arise from the griefs of man and the silence of
God he brings a quiet but profound under-

standing and a healing touch. His treatment
covers all the mysterious, wistful places where
the wind of the Spirit stirs the reed that is man,
and nearly every ford where the soul's weak-
ness wrestles with the eternal strength, except
perhaps the ford that is called Jabbok. The
light of a penetrative but reverent comprehension plays over all he says. Undramatic in
form, he has much of the dramatist's art, much
of his sensitiveness to human fate, of his swift
understanding of human sin and sorrow. And
with this there goes a very instant and vital
sense of the presence of God in human life.[1]

As an estimate of Dr. Hutton—except the
last part of it—such a passage is not only
superficial and inadequate, but actually unjust.
At any rate, it was very unlike the image of
him which I had formed from reading his
books, all of which I had followed with joy
and gratitude. Certainly the unhappy and
misused word "clever" is the last word I should
have thought of applying to him. As far back
as 1904 I read his *Guidance from Robert
Browning in Matters of Faith;* and to this day
I do not know a better exposition of the message of that glorious singer of the triumph of
faith. Later, in 1906, I read his *Pilgrims in*

[1] *Voices of Today,* by Hugh Sinclair.

the Region of Faith, discussing Amiel, Tolstoy, Pater, and Newman; a study in temperament, showing how difficult faith is for introspective, self-analysing minds in an unsettled, all-questioning age. It revealed an incomparable interpreter of spiritual experience as disclosed in great literature, a field in which much of his best service has been rendered. Nothing better has been written about Walter Pater, and no one has come nearer capturing the secret of Newman, whose elusive, if not inscrutable, personality is as baffling as it is fascinating. Those essays prepared me for his brilliant studies of Nietzsche, Chesterton, Ibsen, and Shaw, in *Ancestral Voices.* As for his sermons, I know them from end to end, from *The Fear of Things* to the latest volume, and regard them as among the most suggestive sermons of our time, richly rewarding alike for their spiritual insight and for their artistic stroke.

But I had never met Dr. Hutton, or heard him preach, until he came down to London for the Thursday noonday service on the day of my Recognition as minister of the City Temple —an event delayed for more than a year by

the exigencies of the war.   It was a memorable
occasion, made so by the genius of the preacher
—who, curiously enough, has a greater fame in
America and a larger hearing in England than
in his own Scotland—and his sermon was one
of the dozen supremely great sermons I have
heard in my life.   The theme, the passion of
the preacher, the posture of the times—when
the idealism of the war was beginning to cool—
and, above all, perhaps the meaning of the day
for me personally, made it unforgettable while
memory holds her throne.   Sitting beside him
in the great white pulpit, I felt the very heart-
beat of the vast congregation as the sermon
went home to each hearer, now with terrible
intensity, now with melting pathos, now with
an intimacy indescribable, as if the preacher
had moved to and fro whispering into each
ear—so truly did our own souls speak to us in
the voice from the pulpit.   As I watched the
audience and listened, it seemed to me that
preaching, at its highest, is the greatest art
known among men, more vivid than architecture, more intimate than music, more persuasive than poetry.   My Diary gives a very
dim picture of that scene, but it offers a differ-

ent estimate of Dr. Hutton from that of his
appraiser in 1912. Having lost one son in
the war, and another wounded in a terrifying
manner, it could no longer be said that the
preacher knew grief and anguish only by
imaginative intuition:

Jan. 18th, 1918:—What a sermon Dr. Hutton preached in the City Temple yesterday,
both for its eloquence and its appropriateness.
He dealt with "The Temptation," that is the
one temptation which sums up all others, in-
cluding that of the minister, to which he
alluded with illuminative understanding. What
is the Great Temptation, faced by Jesus in the
wilderness and escaped by none of the sons of
men? It is the cynical spirit, by which we are
sorely tried in these days, and will be more
terribly tried later, because it haunts all high
moods. Subtly, artfully, it seeks to lower,
somehow, the lights of the soul, to slay ideals,
to betray and deliver us to base-mindedness.
Satan, said the preacher, is the base-minded
spirit; he is the denier, as God is the Affirmer,
within all souls. Such preaching! He searches
like a surgeon and heals like a physician.
Seldom, if ever, have I had a man walk right
into my heart with a lighted candle in his hand,
as he did, and look into the dark corners. For
years I had known Dr. Hutton as a master of
the inner life, whether dealing with the Bible

At Close Quarters, or with the friends and aiders of faith, like Browning; and there are passages in *The Winds of God* that haunt me like great music. And no book in this dark time of war—in which, alas, the author has suffered his share of bitter loss—has gripped me more firmly, more surely, than his *Loyalty, the Approach to Faith.* There one hears not the great guns behind dim horizons, but their echo in the lonely places of the soul. As a guide to those who are walking in the middle years of life, where bafflements of faith are many and moral pitfalls are deep, there is no one like Hutton; no one to stand alongside him. Rich as his books are, his preaching is much more wonderful than his writings. His style is indeed a marvel, but one does not think of it while he is preaching. While his sermon has the finish of a literary essay, it is delivered with the enthusiasm of an evangelist. The whole man goes into it, uniting humour, pathos, poetry and hard reason, literature, life, unction, with a certain wildness of abandon, as of one possessed, which is the note of truly great preaching. In my humble judgment he is the greatest preacher in Britain.

The sermon was published—alas, only in part, whole sections of it having been impromptu—in a volume entitled *Our Only Safeguard;* but like most printed sermons, it lacks the inspiration of the occasion and the transfiguration of personality. The sermon was read, as is the usual—though not invariable—habit of the preacher; but for the last twenty minutes he forgot his manuscript entirely, and plunged into the dark forest of Russian literature—which he has studied more profoundly than any man in the modern pulpit —to the heart-shaking scene in the fifth chapter of the fifth book of *The Brothers Karamazov,* by Dostoevsky, where the spirit of anti-Christ, incarnated in the Grand Inquisitor, is face to face with Christ. The faces of the audience seemed ashy grey as they saw the Christ-spirit grapple with ultimate Evil wearing the robes of the church. It made the very soul shiver. The sentences of the preacher flashed like lightning. He crouched behind the pulpit, his face livid with all the sinister suggestions of the scene, as the cool, cunning Spirit of Evil defied Christ in his own name! As a commentary on the temptation of Jesus, which he had taken for his text, it was overwhelming. Then his whole being lighted up as he saw, and made all who heard him see, the incredible might of the Spirit of Love which, on the cross, revealed a power equal to the darkest tragedy and the most desperate temptation of human life. After the service, to an eager group in the vestry, he discoursed of Russia and its spiritual history and message. His knowledge of all things Russian was amazing, and his talk about it was one of the wonders of conversational genius.

Often it has been said that Dr. Hutton—like F. W. Robertson—is a preacher to preachers; and that is true indeed, but in many other senses than the saying usually implies. To go through any of his many volumes, with their instinct for the right subject and their fertile actuality of treatment—their wealth of spiritual insight, intellectual surprise, and literary grace—is at once to understand why so many preachers are keen students of him. He suggests to them the kind of theme they find it worthwhile to talk about, and, without abrogating the necessity of their own thought, he sets their minds travelling on all kinds of stimulating roads. Everywhere he goes he opens doors, and there is hardly a page on which he does not set a lighted candle down beside some dark text, or some dark experience, and leave

it burning. But he does more. It was a saying
of Joseph Parker that any man who preaches
to broken hearts preaches to the times; and in
the widest and profoundest sweep of that spirit
Dr. Hutton preaches to the times in which we
live. Not only does he bring to our troubled
age the grace of insight and the comfort of
great ideas, but he reads the signs of the age
as few men are able to do. For skilled, pene-
trating diagnosis of present-day symptoms—
as in his volume, *Discerning the Times*—he
is one of our first men; and there is no flimsy
sentimentalism or superficiality about his pre-
scriptions, which is another way of saying that
he sets "the times" in the perspective of Time,
linking passing moods and events with abiding
realities.

Few people realise how much the man in the
pulpit preaches to himself, and what a struggle
goes on in his heart in respect of the faith that
makes us men. With some it is a moral
struggle, with some temperamental obscura-
tions, with some intellectual difficulties; and
not a few men of saintly character have remained uncertain to the end. They walked by
faith, not by knowledge. "Rabbi" Duncan, of

Edinburgh, called himself to the last an intellectual sceptic. Life had for him on one side
a precipice, down to the abysses, but on the
other side his feet were on the rock; and that
rock was experience. It is still a matter of
debate whether Newman was not in intellect a
sceptic, as in heart he was a mystic. Even a
casual student of Joseph Parker must feel in
him the stress of a struggle never adjourned—
"an atheism within a theism," as he called it—
and if he did not become a saint, he had it in
him to be a thorough-going sceptic, as well as
a great sinner. So it is with Dr. Hutton, in
whom one finds so little of that over-belief
which to men who live in the thick of things
often sounds like cant, or else like a fourth
dimension.[2] Such struggles make him a helper
of others who are not strong swimmers, and if
he has great compassion it is because he knows

[2] This does not mean that Dr. Hutton is in his heart a
sceptic,—far from it!—but simply that he knows the nature
of faith, and prefers its risk and peril and moral urgency to
the paralysis of dead certainty; as the Pope, in *The Ring and
the Book*, prayed to be delivered from "the torpor of assurance." His position is well set forth in "Further Thoughts from
my Note-book on Newman," which appears as an addendum to
his *Pilgrims of Faith*. Faith stands midway between denial
and credulity, both of which mean the end of adventure and
entreaty. Dr. Hutton agrees with Emerson when he said that
God has given us the choice "between truth and repose,"
whereas half the modern world is seeking repose.

that every man fights a hard fight—often against heavy odds.

One does not wonder at the enthusiasm of Dr. Hutton for Browning, which permeated so much of his earlier preaching and writing. Like that mighty poet, he, too, sees with un- flinching eye the risk and adventure of faith, the pathos and peril of our mortal strife, vividly aware of the contradictions and des- perate enigmas which life flings in the teeth of the soul. He, too, sees life as one might see a man from whom one expected kindness and friendship doing brutal, outrageous things, and offering closed lips and averted eyes to all demands for an explanation. The man is an enemy, then, and we are at his mercy?

"Hush, I pray you!
What if this friend happen to be—God?"

To know the meaning of that "Hush" in his own heart, to be able to say it convincingly, so that a man who is being buffeted and blud- geoned by hard lot, or beshadowed by deep grief, can believe it and take hope—surely that is the highest service which a man can render to his fellows. Of that finest of all arts Dr.

Hutton is a master; he knows how to comfort
men in the true sense, that is, not merely to
soothe, but to strengthen, fortify, establish. At
any rate, no man living can preach to me as he
can, in certain moods, doubly so when he pins
me to the wall and forces me to face the facts
of the moral life, bringing to bear his power
of spiritual analysis, his gift for tracking the
subtler movements of the soul, its hidden
motives, its push and pull of resolution, its blind
thoughts we know not nor can name, and what
Woolman called "the stop in the mind."

For the same reason that Dr. Hutton lent his
soul to Browning in the earlier years, he now
turns to the great Russians, and especially to
Dostoevsky, whom he regards as the profoundest spiritual genius of recent centuries   The
Russians, he thinks, come near to forming an
exception to the law that no man can see God
and live.   Some of them have almost seen Him
and have lived to tell what they saw.   The last
time I heard him he had been reading a Russian book in which it seemed that the last truth
of things was revealed with a thoroughness
and unflinchingness of which we in the West
are incapable.   The book itself was a huddled

and tumultuous business, apparently without
plot, the interest being created and sustained by
the sharpness of the author's psychology. The
writer—whose name he did not give—had
created a truly wonderful effect by making all
his characters run away from the things which
they knew and acknowledged to be perfectly
true. Looking superficially at the book, one
would say that it was disjointed, unstable, and
futile, but beneath the surface it held a lesson
which few western writers could enforce.
Christ was not mentioned in the book from first
to last, but nevertheless he pervaded the whole
of it, as he does so much of Russian literature,
just as Julius Cæsar, while making only a
fugitive appearance in the Shakespeare play
of that title, is felt in every line of it. From
such a delineation of the unmentioned but
acknowledged Christ, from whom men run
away in fear, not of him, but of themselves, he
made us understand how even now, in spite of
its apparent rejection of him, Christ is over-
coming the world. A book by Dr. Hutton—
and his friends will never let him rest until
he writes it—interpreting the soul of Russia in
its literature, and most of all the Russian ex-

perience of Christ, would introduce us to a new
home of ideas—ideas, too, of such a kind that
they may yet heal this tortured world of ours
as with a balm.[3]

It is a criticism of Dr. Hutton, and also a

[3] Since this essay was written Dr. Hutton has published his
lectures on preaching—"conversations," he prefers to call
them—delivered to divinity students at Aberdeen, Edinburgh,
and Glasgow, under the title, *That the Ministry be not Blamed.*
It is a brilliant book, rich in personal revelation, and if one
may not follow all the methods he recommends—as to reading,
for example—he may well be tenacious of methods which
have been so fruitful in his own ministry. More than once he
speaks of "the Great Russians who know everything, and who
know so much about the soul of man indeed that our most
subtle minds, minds like Meredith's even, seem heavy and
half awake." His indebtedness to Browning is celebrated
with rejoicing gratitude, in a passage which is also a plea
for the ministry as a vocation:

"Surely it is no time for a sensitive man who knows history,
and who knows his own soul, to hesitate on the threshold
of this ancient career. Probably never in the history of man
was the great and final question about life at stake as it is
today. All our questions fall back upon deeper questions, and
these on deeper still, until they pause before the great and
Awful question as to what this life of ours means. Are we
human beings irrelevant to this vast system which was our
cradle and becomes our grave? Or is there a blessed hypothesis which thinking, feeling men can honourably hold—a
hypothesis which without robbing life of its mystery and
awe ends for us its aching ambiguity? May we speak
to men of God? There is one solving word for this universe:
it is God. There is one solving word for God: it is Christ.

I am sorry for you men that you have no great poet, as
we had, to set your Christian blood leaping, and disposing you
almost to dance before the Lord. We had Browning: for
whom be all thanks to God for ever and for ever. And
Browning spent his whole life and wrote seventeen volumes
to this and no other effect:

While I see day succeed the deepest night—
How can I speak but as I know?—my speech
Must be, throughout the darkness, 'It will end:
The light that did burn, will burn!' "

tribute to him, that, rich as his sermons and essays are, they seem too much like by-products to be accepted as his final contribution to the religious thought of his time. All his friends feel that he has it in him to do some great thing in behalf of the life of faith—a thing which no one else can do—and for this they are waiting. So rare a blend of spiritual and literary resource, so unique a gift of insight and expression, which have given him an influence and power such as few preachers can command, ought to be employed at full stretch on the problems to which the modern mind is so sensitive. The best promise of a fulfilment of this demand, so far, is his series of lectures on *The Proposal of Jesus,* which sets the life and ministry of the Master in a new and revealing light. It is one of the most fruitful books of recent times, suggestive even in its discursiveness, and one which no one can read without feeling anew that the hope of the world is that we may yet discover what Christianity is. In this discovery and interpretation of the religion of Jesus, Dr. Hutton, now in the prime and splendour of his powers—richly endowed, radiant in his insight and personality—ought

to have a great part. He himself, with that
divination of the deeper trend of things which
is so marked a trait of his genius, feels that
we are on the eve of unpredictable revelations
and advances in the faith and fortune of our
humanity. As we may read in a passage of
which I am fond:

"I sometimes think that in a great, wholesale
way we are all of us about to make a wonderful discovery. At times it seems to me as
though we were on the edge and moment of a
world-shaking revolution in thought and mood.
For a long time now we have been feeling our
way in a vast, unlit corridor, contending with
others in the dark, striking out at shapes which
seem to be wishing to do us harm, when all the
time they, like ourselves, may only have been
out upon their business, and, like us, in the
dark. I sometimes think that in answer to the
cry of our present distress a light is once more
about to shine: and by this light we shall see
again an open door, and beyond this door the
fair earth and sky. I sometimes think that
we are all of us on the point of making the
discovery that our Christianity is true, and that
for mankind to oppose it or neglect it, is for
mankind in the long run—and a long run is
needed for the testing of principles—to rush
down a steep place and to perish."

III. Dean Inge, of St. Paul's

At a meeting of the Whitefriars Club one night Dean Inge read an essay on immortality. It was an able essay, of course, albeit so abstract and difficult to follow that it left the company puzzled, if not depressed. The eternal hope seemed as remote as a star, as vague as a dream, and so attenuated as to be hardly desirable at all. No one had the courage to start the discussion, until Bernard Shaw made bold to say that having lived sixty years, or thereabouts, he was not encouraged to go on by such a prospect. It was too awful to contemplate, and he proceeded to advocate the organisation of a Suicide Club. The essay, or an elaboration of it, appeared in *Outspoken Essays*—one of the few books of our day which will be read fifty years hence—and the impish attitude of Shaw, who is never more happy than when he can gibe a dean or a bishop, may be inferred from his review of that volume. Among other saucy things, he said:

These essays, dazzling as they are, have done much to confirm me in a conviction which has been deepening in me for years, that what we call secondary education as practised in our public schools and universities is destructive to any but the strongest minds, and even to them is disastrously confusing. I find in the minds of all able and original men and women who have been so educated, a puzzling want of homogeneity. They are full of chunks of un-assimilated foreign bodies which are more troublesome and dangerous than the vacancies I find in the minds of those who have not been educated at all. I prefer a cavity to a cancer or a calculus: it is capable of being filled with healthy tissue and is not malignant. In the mind of the dean, which is quite unmistakably a splendid mind, I find the most ridiculous sub-stances, as if, after the operation of educating him, the surgeon-pedagogue had forgotten to remove his sponges and instruments and sewn them up inside him.

There is no doubt that Dean Inge is one of the greatest minds on the British Isles; but if his thinking does not give one quite the im-pression of hopeless confusion which Shaw de-scribed, it does set one wondering over that extraordinary bundle of antinomies we call the human intellect. An aristocrat by nature and training, he has the knack of catching the ear

of the crowd, as much by the vivid colors he
employs as by the challenge of his thought. If
not actually a pessimist in his temperament, he
is at least a Cassandra—doomed to tell the
bitter truth and have nobody believe it—whose
dismal outlook entitles him to be called "the
gloomy dean," a title given as a reward for his
remarkable lectures on *The Church and the
Age*. One such prophet, if no more, is needed
in every generation, and we are sorely in need
of one in America, if only to mitigate our easy,
evasive optimism which plays ostrich in the
face of dark facts. A great Christian teacher,
the dean seems to contradict in one breath what
he says in the next; so much so that the
Methodist Times, after reading his Romanes
Lecture on *Progress,* was moved to ask:
"Has Dean Inge heard of the gospel?" A
rationalist who relegates miracles to "the
sphere of pious opinion," he is an apostle of a
lofty, if somewhat severe, spirituality; and at
the very moment when one expects his shrewd,
positive mind to be dogmatic, he "slips through
the stile of religious imagination to gather
moon-flowers betwixt dusk and dawn."

The surprise was general when the dean

chose Christian mysticism as the theme of his Bampton Lectures; and if at first reading he did not seem to get beyond the fringe of the subject, interest soon shifted from the thesis to the personality of the author. It was astonishing that one of his type of mind, who apparently had not the slightest suspicion that "they see not clearest who see all things clear," should undertake such a study. But a further reading revealed an odd mixture of rationalism and spiritual immediacy, and in spite of his criticisms of the excesses and excrescences of mysticism, the sober web of his thought was shot through with the glow and fire of the reality he sought to expound. Since that time there have been many manuals of mysticism, some wise, some not wise. Evelyn Underhill is scholarly, weighty, noble, though a mediævalist; E. Herman is worth looking into, albeit too much inclined to cleverness—like a juggler doing tricks with the Pearl of Eternity. The great masterpiece in exposition of mysticism in our day is *The Way of Divine Union*, by A. E. Waite, who writes from the inside and with the winged wisdom of a poet, as one who has in his experience that which gives him the key

to much that is hidden from others. But Dean
Inge led the way in the study of mysticism, and
it is his subtle, shy affinity with the mystics that
makes him a worthy successor to a great
dynasty of deans, and the one voice to which all
England listens.

As a preacher Dean Inge is singularly effective, if one forgets the most amazing
mannerisms ever seen in a pulpit, and attends
to the matter of his discourse. With clear-cut,
ascetic face, scholarly in bearing, looking taller
than he is, he has a sober, dry-eyed, didactic
personality, and an elocution atrocious in its
angularity. As he rises to read his sermon—
often without noticing that the audience is
present—that straight, level, self-contained
look makes no appeal, and the thin, flexible lips
seem made to set inferior folk right on no very
gentle terms. He makes little concession to
dulness or ignorance. As he reads on, his
facial expression suggests a contortionist, as
he launches his clear, carrying voice—rather
rasping at times, owing, no doubt, to his deaf-
ness—into the vast spaces of the cathedral.
His attitude is one of aristocratic carelessness,
as if he trusted to the vaults and pillars to bear

his message, but is not greatly concerned whether they do or not. His matter is a compound of epigram and paradox, or mordant wit and rapier-like satire, matching the tartness of his tones. His humour is of the intellectual variety, and more often than not with a sting in its tail. Without wasting a word, in a style as incisive as his thought—clear, concise, keen-cutting—he sets forth the truth as he sees it. There is no unction in his preaching, no pathos. It is cold intellect, with never a touch of tenderness. Much of what he says is more able than weighty, more brilliant than moving, leaving one wiser rather than better, abashed rather than lifted. Yet, at rare intervals, in the middle of a lecture, there is sometimes a brief unveiling, and one sees the prophet-soul behind the superficial habit of sardonic criticism and pungent epigram.

So the Dean of St. Paul's stands before us with his dry, biting speech, his formidable sarcasm, his alarming air of finality, his startling gift of characterisation, and even in his gentlest moods one feels a bleak wind round the corner. It would not do for all preachers to be of his order. Men need comfort as well as

castigation. Yet what austere sincerity is his,
what intrepid courage, what weight of clear
judgment, what prophetic power! His quality
is that of the Hebrew prophets, with more of
Jeremiah than of Isaiah in his spiritual outlook,
and if he inspires less affection than any great
preacher of his time, it is due partly to his forbidding temperament, but chiefly to his habit of
exploding shams and absurdities. Using the
flail of John the Baptist, he is a gift of God to
our age with its "Lo, here" and "Lo, there,"
and every kind of fad runs rife. The dean is
unconcerned about majorities, impervious to
popular feeling. Indeed, one suspects that he
is uncomfortable in a majority, like the elder
statesman who, when his speech was applauded
by the multitude, asked uneasily, "Have I said
anything very foolish?" Anyway, he holds
it to be a maxim that "the church can rarely
co-operate with a popular movement," by which
he means that it can seldom tread the path of
success, and never because it is the path of success. Unfortunately his bald veracity is not
graced by the genius of speaking the truth in
love, and he utters hard sayings regardless of
consequences; but he will not compromise his

gospel. During the Great War, when so many churchmen of all communions took low ground, he never mitigated by one iota the severity of the Christian message. Later, when so many pandered to the growing power of the labour movement, the dean stood firm, refusing to weaken his gospel in the service of a political party. It did not matter that he was denounced as an obstinate obscurantist; he upheld the dignity of a faith which commands, and can never be subject to the experiences of the hour.

Every right-thinking man must honour the dean for his unyielding tenacity to principle; but at times he seems to stand so straight that he leans backward. Even before he has uttered a word against it one knows that he despises democracy and has no faith in it, because it smells of the mob. Certainly he does not believe that the majority is right, much less that massed ignorance makes wisdom. Often he seems to identify democracy with socialism, if not with demagogy, and he smites both with the swift sword of his satire. Not that he is opposed to social reform. He would indeed build the City of God "in England's green and pleasant land"; but always with the tools of the spirit. Nor does this attitude mean, as his critics are so ready to infer, that Christianity should be the fortress and bulwark of aristocracy. Far from it. His point is that the church must be ready, if need be, to incur the antagonism of old aristocracy and the vituperations of young demos alike, truckling to neither. She must not cringe to the masses in our day as she once did to the classes; must not seek to be applauded by a multitude who demanded the crucifixion of her Master, and could demand it again—that is the core of a message delivered with needless acerbity, invective and scorn. It is a sound message and one sorely needed in our day, unpalatable though it be. But like all men of wisdom, the dean has his defects, his blind spots, the chief of which— as one might have guessed—is an incredible astigmatism with respect to the social meaning and application of Christianity. Take, for example, his lecture on "The Kingdom of God in the World," and one feels that the gibe of Bernard Shaw was well nigh justified.

Can we point to any recognisable type of character and belief and say, This is Christianity? We might try. Say that belief in the fatherhood of God, in the brotherhood of man, in the sacredness and eternal importance of the essential part of each personality; the immeasurable superiority of moral goodness to any worldly advantages; love as the crown of all the virtues; selfishness as the root of sin; hypocrisy, hard-heartedness and prudent worldliness as the three things our Lord hated most, trust in God and joy even in affliction; the simple life; the love of wisdom; accumulations of money a snare to their owner; the great renunciation,—he that will save his life shall lose it, and he that will lose his life shall save it—and what Matthew Arnold calls the method of inwardness—these do seem to be enough for a fairly clear notion of what a real Christian is like, and in considering the influence of Christianity on the social order this is also important: that the gospel works by personal influence upon the will and affections and not by external machinery. Jesus left no book, no code, no system: he wrote his gospel on the hearts of men. A slow method? Yes, it is a slow method: it is not easy to change people, but that was the method he chose—like the ancient torch race in which the wearied runner handed on his torch to someone else to carry on. The Christian religion is not taught; it is caught from someone who has it.

The preaching of this gospel is and always has been the great business of the church. All Christians must agree in combating, for ex-

ample, all exploitation and ruining of souls
all that great network of co-operative guilt
with limited liability which makes up so much
of secular society. But when we are invited
to go further and take sides as a church in matters in which good and wise men are divided,
the case is different. I am not suggesting for
a moment that Christians should not have
political opinions. I am speaking of organised
Christianity as such, and I say deliberately that
Christians ought not to organise themselves
as Christians for any particular social or
political propaganda. We do not want a powerful political church again, whether run by
Catholics or Independents. Christianity is a
leaven, it can never be more. Our Lord made
that absolutely plain, that he never expected to
have the majority on his side. Our Lord never
gave any reason to suppose the church would
ever be successful in winning the masses as
such. He never gave any reason to think there
would ever be an inconvenient crowd gathered
round the narrow gate. Therefore all this kind
of clerical demagogy and democracy is fundamentally contrary to his method, and it is,
though many good people think otherwise, a
treachery against his teaching.

There we have it "plain and flat," as Lowell
would say; on the one side a powerful political
church to be avoided, and on the other not even
a co-operative conscience with limited liability

to match the organised iniquity of the world. In short, every protest of the church against political infamy, every effort of Christians—other than individual—in behalf of juster, wiser, more merciful laws, every attempt of the pulpit to translate the teachings of Jesus into practical social justice is, as Dean Inge sees it under the glorious dome of St. Paul's, a form of treachery and demagogy. "What can we do?" is surely a fair question, and the dean answers it in his closing lecture on "The Church and the Age," from which we learn, after a merciless flaying of nearly every forward-looking movement of our time, that "the whole duty of the church is to hold up the Christian view of life, the Christian standard of values, steadily before the eyes" of the people, laying emphasis upon love, sympathy, economy, sincerity, holy living, "setting a good example" for the poorer members of our own class, and indirectly for "the class below," upon charity, prayer, and the duty of helping to form a moral public opinion against the evils of foolish fashions, gambling, and the like. More specifically, three avenues of influence seem to be open to Christian enterprise, three modern tendencies with which "we, as church people, may co-operate and assist." They are the breaking down of class barriers, the spread of education, and the care of public health, and especially the support of the new science of eugenics! Such is the programme of the Christian church, as outlined in the old grey cathedral of England, at a time when the world is shattered by universal war, disfigured by industrial brutality, plundered by greed, and staggering under the shadow of a vast despair! One recalls the word of Carlyle: "The world asks of its church in these times, more passionately than of any other institution, the question—Canst thou teach us or not?"

Howbeit, my purpose here is not to argue with Dean Inge, but simply to portray his outlook and art as a preacher. He stands for a point of view—held by many noble and true hearted men—which, if held by all, would make the church an *arcana celestia* of a barren and immovable conservatism; but that is not the attitude of the church of today and it never will be! Jesus was not put to death for laying emphasis upon love, sympathy, prayer, and the doing of good, but for making a definite pro-

posal for the public policy of the world; and
if following him leads the church to Calvary,
it is not better than its leader.   For the character, the scholarship, and the noble prophetic
courage of Dean Inge, we give thanks, but we
refuse to follow him in his advocacy of "the
public impotence of religion."   His fame will
outlive his defects, and the stones he has laid
will abide as a foundation for other and perhaps more genial workers.   One such stone is
his vision of a church truly one, not in organisation or creed or ritual, but because drawn to
communion through a profound veneration and
love for its Master.   He has taught us out of
long and deep study that the mystics all tell
the same tale; all climb the same mountain, and
their witness agrees together.   All ages, all
sects, all languages are blended harmoniously
on that shining Jacob's ladder which scales the
heavens in far other fashion than was ever
dreamed of by the builders of Babel.   Despite
the deflections of his insight, he has interpreted
that eternal religion which is the original divine
poetry, whereof our theologies are imperfect
translations, summing it up in a golden passage
which Bernard Shaw was "wicked" enough to

say is one of the rare intervals of inspiration enjoyed by the dean in the midst of the years:

It allows us what George Meredith calls "the rapture of the forward view." It brings home to us the meaning of the promise of Christ that there are many things yet hid from humanity which will in the future be revealed by the Spirit of Truth. It encourages us to hope that for each individual who is trying to live the right life the venture of faith will be progressively justified in experience. It breaks down the denominational barriers which divide men and women who worship the Father in spirit and in truth—barriers which become more senseless in each generation, since they no longer correspond even approximately with real differences of belief or of religious temperament. It makes the whole world kin by offering a pure religion which is substantially the same in all climates and in all ages— a religion too divine to be fettered by any man-made formulas, too nobly human to be readily acceptable to men in whom the ape and tiger are still alive, but which finds a congenial home in the purified spirit which is the throne of the Godhead. Such is the type of faith which is astir among us. It makes no imposing show in church conferences; it does not fill our churches and chapels; it has no organisation, no propaganda; it is for the most passively loyal, without much enthusiasm, to the institutions among

which it finds itself. But in reality it has over-
leapt all barriers; it knows its true spiritual
kin; and amid the strifes and perplexities of
a sad, troublous time it can always cover its
hope and confidence by ascending in heart and
mind to the heaven which is closer to it than
breathing, and nearer than hands and feet.

IV: Charles E. Jefferson

It so happened that I heard Dr. Jefferson
preach just after I had read his four golden
books of counsel and guidance in the matter of
preaching.[1] It was an interesting experience,
like listening to a master painter lecture
on painting, and then watching him paint a picture; and never did practice fulfil precept more
perfectly. Those four books, if taken together,
form the best course of practical instruction
for a young minister with which I am acquainted, as much for their fraternal spirit as
for their plain-spoken wisdom. They have the
ring of reality, the tang of experience, as of
one who is not spinning a theory but telling us
what he has learned by living. Uniting a
heavenly vision with homely common sense,
they show us how, since we have this treasure

[1] *The Minister as Shepherd* and *The Minister as Prophet*
were lectures delivered at the Bangor Theological Seminary;
The Building of the Church was the Yale lectures for 1910;
while *Quiet Hints to Growing Preachers* is a series of familiar
talks in the study, telling things that laymen need not hear.

in earthen vessels, we must make the vessel fit
for the divine use. A little book long famous
in English literature was entitled *A Mirror
for Magistrates;* and these books are a Mirror for Ministers, showing the things that help
and the faults that mar the ministry—a mirror held in a wise and brotherly hand.

Some of us regard *The Building of the
Church* as one of the best of all the historic
series of Yale Lectures, if only because it approaches the preacher through the church.
There we see the preacher against the background of "organised preaching" in which his
labor is enshrined; in the environment of faith
and prophecy of which he is both the creation
and the interpreter. The thesis of the lectures,
expounded with characteristic lucidity of insight and style, is that preaching involves not
one man only, but a society of men and women.
The sermon does not grow out of the soul of
the preacher alone, but out of the deep heart
of the church. It is not the preacher who
makes the church; it is the church which makes
the preacher. He does not shape himself, but
is moulded by the communal life and faith of
a body of believers, and gives back what he

receives. The church in her corporate experience is his mother, to whom he owes his life
of faith, and, by the same token, a life of loyalty. He is not an isolated individual, but an
organ functioning in an organism; and his
ministry belongs to him not alone by virtue of
his temperament, his poetic gift, or his social
passion, but as an endowment of the church of
God whose son and servant he is.

With this thesis fresh in my mind, when I
entered the "Skyscraper Church," as the
Broadway Tabernacle is called by the New
York papers, I felt that I was approaching
Dr. Jefferson through the great church which,
in its present form and influence, is the creation of his faith as a leader and his acumen as
an executive, no less than of his genius as a
preacher. When he came to New York in 1898
he found a church living almost wholly in the
past, and stifling in a neighbourhood quite un-
favourable to growth. He made certain demands as conditions of his acceptance—there
was, I am told, a three months' option clause,
long since forgotten by both pastor and people
—and from that uncertain beginning, in spite
of the swelling tides of alien populations, and

the swiftly shifting conditions of New York, the church has grown, and the preacher has grown with it, until today it is a bulwark of righteousness, a shrine of faith and a throne of power, in the greatest city of America. If Emerson was right when he said that every institution is the lengthened shadow of a man, the building at Fifty-sixth Street, with its modern appointments and equipment, and still more the noble Christian community, whose gracious, wholesome, creative activities take so many forms of fruitful service, is the incarnation of the spirit, personality and constructive vision of its minister. Such a ministry, so wisely and quietly wrought, rich in insight and enterprise, deserves to be celebrated with gratitude and joy by the whole church of every name.

The New York papers are wont to describe Dr. Jefferson as stern, cold, unbending, an old-time Puritan pastor in whose thought modernism has no place, and whose methods are as masterful as his personality. It is a strange caricature, as alien to the spirit of the preacher as it is unlike the Puritans whose history he knows as few others. He does embody the

heroic Puritan tradition, and if there is any
place on earth where such a minister is needed
more than another, it is in our gay and giddy-
paced metropolis, in the garish glitter of
Broadway. They err who think him stern,
cold, or unbending; though, as he sits in the
pulpit, his appearance does give one an impression of firmness, if not of austerity. But as he
begins to speak his rugged face is illumined
by an inner brightness, and one discovers that
it is the firmness of strength, of poise, of seren-
ity, suffused by a great gentleness, and touched
by that elusive magnetic quality so impossible
to define. On that long-gone Sunday morning
the Tabernacle was full, the men outnumber-
ing the women—young men, especially, to
whom the preacher is so attractive. If, as
Delsarte once said, "mediocrity is not the too
little, but the too much," Dr. Jefferson is a
genius in the conduct of public worship. The
service was simple, natural, satisfying, rich
without being ornate, reverent without being
formal; and it did what every service of social
worship is intended to do. It welded an audience into a congregation, wooing us out of our

lonely isolation into liberty and joy of fellowship.

The sermon had to do with the atonement, and I felt a sense of dismay when he announced the theme, expecting a dull time with an old theological riddle. Having used the word once or twice, he threw it aside, because of the unrealities associated with it, using, instead, the word "reconciliation," which is nearer to the experience of the New Testament. As a thinker it was plain that he stood in the tradition of Clement of Alexandria, and, later, of Schleiermacher, Maurice, Wordsworth, and Coleridge, to whom the incarnation was "the climax of immanence in the world," and the atonement an age-long process in which God is ever present and all-suffering. The old ideas of the atonement, he said, were either artificial, mechanical, or theatrical. The idea of God underlying them was not only inadequate, but false. Henceforth we must think in terms of fatherhood, drawing our analogies not from the courthouse and the counting-room, but from the deepest, holiest realities of life. Quite frankly the preacher gave us more than one glimpse of the struggle in his own heart in days agone, and how he rebelled against the old dogma: "I would not accept it. I became an infidel. No man can accept a doctrine that darkens his moral sense. I wonder in telling this if I have not spoken the experience of many of you this morning." Indeed, yes. Some of us knew every footprint along that dark path, and the bitter agony of the way. He told how a minister, who had outgrown the old dogmas, led him to see a clearer vision which set his heart singing. No doubt it was Phillips Brooks, under whose spell he fell as a young man, and by whom he was won from the law to the ministry. What a lawyer he would have made, with his clear incisive intellect, his scrupulous precision as a workman, and his gift of quiet, persuasive eloquence! Another bit of self-revelation came in his reply to those who say that, if God carries the wound of the world in his heart, He cannot be happy: "Of course he cannot be happy. Children are happy, grown people never are. After we have passed over the days of childhood, there is happiness no longer. Some of us have lived too long and borne too much ever to be happy any more." An undertone of pathos, far enough from pessimism—as of one whom the years has taken below the surface of things, some way down into the mystery and sorrow of life—made itself heard all through the sermon, if the ear that listened was sensitive. It was real preaching, what the English call "preaching of the centre," heart speaking to heart in words so simple that one felt the impact of reality. Somehow it recalled a passage in one of his lectures in which he tells what a sermon costs, and how the preacher must live the word of God before he preaches it:

A sermon is not a manufactured product, but a spiritual creation. It is not a machine which a man can construct in his sermonic shop, and set running in the pulpit like the electric toys which one sees sometimes on the corner of the city street. A sermon is an exhalation, a spiritual vapor emerging from the oceanic depths of the preacher's soul. It is an emanation, an efflux, an effluence flowing from an interior fountain hidden in the depths of personality. It is an efflorescence, an outflowing of beautiful things whose home is in the blood. It is a perfume from spiritual roses blooming in the garden of the heart. It is a fruit growing on the tree of a man's life. "A good tree cannot bring forth evil fruit, neither can a corrupt tree bring forth good fruit." Make the tree good.

A sermon is the life-blood of a Christian spirit. A preacher dies in the act of preaching. He lays down his life for his brethren. He saves others, himself he cannot save. The pulpit is a Golgotha in which the preacher gives his life for the life of the world. Preaching is a great work. To do it as God wants it done, the preacher must be a good man, full of the Holy Ghost and of faith.[2]

There are those who hold that oratory always moves on a more or less low moral plane, and is an exercise perilous alike to the soul of speaker and hearer. Froude, who could not do away with eloquence, thought it nearly always misleading, if not dishonest; and Montaigne was of a similar opinion. Meredith has an epigram sufficiently light, to the effect that oratory "is always the more impressive for the spice of temper which renders it untrustworthy." [3] Dr. Jefferson shares this distrust of oratory—he so fears unreality—and that, too, in spite of his amazing gift of lucid, fitly coloured, gracious and moving speech. He knows how easily an orator is betrayed into saying more than he sees, mistaking ornament for

[2] *The Building of the Church,* Lecture VIII.
[3] *Diana of the Crossways,* Chap. i.

insight; a peril which, if unchecked, eats away the moral fibre of a man. He knows that if a man sets out to be eloquent, using oratorical tricks, stratagems and pyrotechnics, he bids good-bye to truth and sincerity. One of his sayings ought to be written in the mind of every young minister: "Never endeavour to be eloquent. It may be that God will let you be eloquent half a dozen times in your life, but I am sure you cannot be eloquent if you try to be." All of which bespeaks the austere integrity of the man, his veracity of soul in dealing with the truth, and with the people. For no one has a more vivid sense of the potent, far-reaching influence of true Christian speech, whose word is also a deed, and of which he is one of the noblest masters among us.

Style, he once said, is perfect when it becomes invisible; and that exactly describes his own style. It puts on no airs, knows no frills, and attracts no attention to itself. It fits his thought as tightly as the skin fits the flesh. There is not a wrinkle, and it is so natural and true that unless you sit before it as a critic and pay close attention, you will not see it at all. Simple, sinewy, flexible, it can preach a serman, write an essay, or tell a lovely Christmas story, with equal grace and ease. The style of a preacher is conditioned, of course, by his mental quality and the fashion of his spoken address. Thus, the stately, sweeping periods of Gunsaulus were suited to the uses of his voice; that magnificent organ whose rich and manifold music follows us down the years. In like manner, the diction of Dr. Jefferson is admirably attuned to the character of his delivery, which is clear, gentle, melodious and of varied modulation. He is sparing of gesture; his sentences are short; his language is rich in colour, but its beauty is inwrought rather than decorative. His sermons are not read, but spoken, and that with an air of the utmost ease and spontaneity—like a teacher telling a tale, like a friend persuading you of a high matter. There is passion in his discourse, but it is not of a kind that resembles a torrent of fire. Rathe., as was said of John Ker—whom he resembles in many ways—it is like "a warm radiance shining through the windows of a home where strong conviction and quiet faith dwell at peace with understanding and hope and acquaintance with grief." He does not

seek to take the mind of an audience by violence or to carry it away on an impetuous tide
of words. His way is rather to win his hearers, taking them captive unawares, showing
them the beauty of the gospel and the meaning
of their lives, seeking to lead them into the freedom and service of the Master.

An English writer has recently said that one
grave fault of the pulpit of our day, and especially in America, is what he picturesquely
calls "suburban preaching." [4] By suburban
preaching he does not mean preaching to people who live in the suburbs, but preaching
which makes its home on the fringes and out-
skirts of Christian truth, rather than in the
centre and the citadel; preaching that has
much to say about the minor moralities, and the
passing events of the day, but very little about
the great themes of the gospel. If, the writer
adds, preachers like Wesley, Newman, Dale,
Spurgeon and Liddon have one common word
to speak to the pulpit of today it is this: that
behind all great preaching there lies always a
great gospel greatly conceived. To that list of
names he might have added Jefferson, whose

[4] Dr. George Jackson, in *The Manchester Guardian*.

plea for doctrinal preaching—as in his lecture
on "The Place of Dogma in Preaching"—has
been fulfilled, in a crowded and versatile ministry, by showing what such preaching should be.
Take any of his volumes, such as *Doctrine
and Deed* and *The New Crusade*—which are
an honour to the American pulpit—and you
find him dealing with the basic issues of faith,
both in their profound significance for thought
and in their practical meaning for life.   His
volume entitled *Things Fundamental* was a
series of Lenten sermons, his custom being to
devote that sacred season not merely to pious
reverie, but to grappling with the great truths
which, like the rock ribs of the earth, underlie
and uphold the lives of all Christian men.   Indeed, in the first sermon I heard him preach
there was a passage as apt today as it was well-
nigh twenty years ago:

If Protestantism today is not doing what it
ought to do, and is manifesting symptoms
which are alarming to Christian leaders, it is
because she has in these recent years been en-
gaged so largely in practical duties as to forget
to drink inspiration from the great doctrines
which must forever furnish life and strength

and hope. If you will allow me to prophesy
this morning I predict that the preaching of the
next fifty years will be far more doctrinal than
the preaching of the last fifty years has been.
I imagine some of you will shudder at that.
You say you do not like doctrinal preaching,
you want preaching that is practical. Well,
pray, what is practical preaching? . . . If
you really want practical preaching, the only
preaching that is deserving the name is preaching that deals with the great Christian doctrines. When people say they do not like doctrinal preaching they often mean that they do
not like preaching which belongs to the seven-
teenth or sixteenth centuries. They are not to
blame for this. There is nothing that gets
stale so soon as preaching. We cannot live on
the preaching of a by-gone age. But doctrinal
preaching need not be antiquated or belated, it
may be fresh, it may be couched in the language
in which men were born. And whenever it
does this there is no preaching which is so
thrilling and uplifting and mighty as that which
deals with the great fundamental doctrines.[5]

Some one has said that any regular attendant at the Broadway Tabernacle could pass an
examination on Christian teaching, both as to
its ruling ideas and their application to the life
of today. It is indeed true, as two recent series

[5] *Doctrine and Deed.*

of sermons may illustrate. One had to do with
"Work and Wages," and dealt with economic
facts and forces in the light of Christian truth,
revealing an astonishing knowledge of facts,
in a spirit as far removed from an erratic radicalism as from a petrified conservativism.
Another series, which ran for more than two
months, was entitled "How to Live," and
showed how well and wisely Dr. Jefferson fulfills what the Catholics call the office of Direc-
tion—that is, specific guidance in the details of
practical spiritual life—which, next to hard
pastoral work, is one of the greatest needs of
the Protestant church. For example, the
church tells men to pray, but it does not tell
them how to do it. The physician must not
simply tell his patients to be well, he must tell
them how to live—how to sleep, what to eat,
and the rest. The church ought to do the same
for the moral and spiritual life. There are
difficulties of course in handling mental and
spiritual hygiene in the pulpit, but people need
help—definite instruction—and if they do not
find it in the church, in their need they will go
elsewhere to get it, perhaps to the mercenary
quack and the half-baked charlatan.

Not alone as a builder of faith and character, but equally in behalf of social justice, the fraternity of classes and the comity of nations, Dr. Jefferson has been a seer-like leader. No preacher in this land has been a more relentless enemy of war, using fact, reason, satire— every weapon in his bright armory—to fight the fiend. Some of his addresses are memorable, as when he led a visitor from Mars upon a tour of the earth, taking him behind the scenes in the parliamentary assemblies of the nations, until, disgusted at the duplicity of mankind—mouthing about peace and making ready for war—to hide his horror the Martian boarded a celestial express for a saner planet! What the world-tragedy meant to Dr. Jefferson, both as a fulfilment of his forebodings and a crucifixion of his ideals, only his brethren who walked through the same valley of shadow can ever know. Not all the casualties of war are on the battlefield; in the hearts of Christian men there is devastation and unspeakable woe. Cast down but not destroyed, saddened but not defeated, Dr. Jefferson sought to interpret the will and truth of God in the awful exegesis of events; hence his volume, *What*

the War has Taught Us. He has been a tower
of strength in days of rancour and reaction,
and often he alone found the needed word for
the hour, as when, on the Sunday following
the rejection of the Covenant of the League
of Nations by the Senate, he took for his text
the words: *"And Noah was drunk."* In a
fairer, juster day men will turn the pages of
his prophetic witness and thank God for a man
who was clear-visioned under a cloudy sky, and
whose testimony for righteousness, no less than
his rebuke of evil, was uttered with gentleness
of heart and the dignity of a golden voice.

Truly it is a great ministry, worthy of
honour in all the churches, its influence more
wide-ranging than the minister himself knows,
and in ways no art can trace. To his younger
brethren—some of whom toil alone in far
places—it is a comfort and joy just to know
that he is there, keeping the light of God aglow
amid the glare of Broadway. His genius as
preacher and pastor is only equalled by his
wealth of friendship, his brotherly kindness,
his sagacity in counsel, and his leadership in
all Christian enterprise. Every man of us

knows that whoever else may lose heart, let go of faith, or lower the ideal of the minister of Christ, that will Dr. Jefferson never! In days when the church is the target of every kind of calumny, and many fall away, he bids us lift up our hearts, remembering the words of the Lord Jesus how he said:

"I will build my church." He is a work. The church is no little private enterprise of ours. It is his. We are colabourers with him. Critics rage and brilliant writers imagine a vain thing. Kings and rulers in divers realms take counsel together and agree that the glory of the church is departing. The Lord holds them in derision. The church is not obsolescent. Humanity has not outgrown it. Its noon is not behind it. Its triumphal career has only begun. We are toiling amid the mists of the early morning. It is the rising sun that smites our foreheads, and we cannot even dream of the victory which is to be. We work upon an enduring institution. After the flags of republics and empires have been blown to tatters and the earth itself has tasted death, the church of Jesus shall stand forth glorious, free from blemish and mark of decay, the gates of Hades shall not prevail against it. Therefore, my beloved brethren, in these confused and confusing days, be steadfast, immovable in the presence of the world's clamour and rancour, always building your life and the lives of as many as God entrusts to your keeping, into the church of the Lord, for as much as you know that such labour is not in vain in the Lord.

V: W. E. Orchard

"I tell you what it is. That parson is city-bred, a town man down to the roots of him. If he'd got the sea and the hills in his soul, or the great wide spaces, and if he heard the cry of the wind above the rattle of your beastly old streets, he'd not say much about the things that seem big to him now, and he'd not know how to say enough about some things he gets rid of in five minutes!"

After such manner a man from the far Back Bush of Australia, who had lived in the great, lonely silences until he had been stripped of all conventionality, but confirmed in the worship and fear of God, spoke of Dr. Orchard in his Enfield days. The man from the Bush never went to church—did not care a hang about it, he said—and at first he was shocked by the sermon, as no anæmic sermon-taster knows how to be shocked. But he soon realised the profound reverence and sincerity of the preacher, despite a seeming flippancy and a love of shocking people, from which he has never recovered. There was a point in the thrust; but it is also true that if Dr. Orchard had the wave in his heart and the cry of the wind in his soul, he would have less to give the restless, nervous, jostled city folk to whom he ministers, and which makes him easily the most picturesque and outstanding figure in the Free Church pulpit of London.

In the stormy days of the New Theology discussion, hardly an echo of which remains, Dr. Orchard stood with R. J. Campbell, albeit with an accent, emphasis and point of view all his own. By virtue alike of temperament and experience both were wandering stars, each in his own orbit, but Orchard was the abler of the two, having a more incisive intellect as well as a finer literary quality. His early thesis upon *Modern Theories of Sin* revealed a man with whom to reckon, at once provocative and provoking in thought, as fearless in criticism as he was fruitful in constructive insight. Many still think that some of the best work he has ever done was as confidant and counsellor of souls astray, torn between sorrow and revolt, whereof we read in *Problems and Perplexi-*

ties—one of the best books of its kind ever written. Indeed, he is reported to have said that it was in dealing with the difficulties of others that he discovered the inadequacy, if not bankruptcy, of the New Theology, and a need for something deeper, more drastic, more real. Hence his "trek back to Christ," as he described it, wherein he abandoned the position then held, or rather went beyond it towards a Free Catholicism. The closing pages of the little book gave a hint of this tendency:

> The true Church is that organism which continues the ministry of Jesus Christ, and is the body of God's increasing incarnation. At present no organisation can be identified with that organism. . . . But it does follow that the present institution can never become the church of God. It will probably grow worse before it grows better. It will have to face reform or extinction. . . . It is impossible to predict the character of the next generation. But there will probably be a change in the very idea of the church, and it is more than likely that the conflicting ideals of Catholicism and Protestantism will disappear and give rise to a fresh synthesis. . . . The church will then be truly catholic, for it will embrace every type: lowly, like the Lord, the servant rather than the mistress, the learner even more than the

teacher. Surely all within the church must
hear the warning sounds. They come not from
the defiant world; the world heeds us not; nor
from some scornful ambassador of the gates of
hell. That sound is the church's Lord, knock-
ing, without!

Even in his liberal days Dr. Orchard was a
liberalist with a difference; as far removed
from an arid rationalism as from the dilettante
whose theology is a confection of rose-water
sentiment. For him Christianity was dynamite, not jam, a stroke of lightning, not a stick
of candy. He held that liberalism meant that
a man was free to be a Christian, not that he
holds his Christianity lightly or loosely; that he
has the same charity toward the past as toward
the future, and is as willing to listen to St.
Bernard as to Henri Bergson. Otherwise, he
said, our boasted liberalism is only sound and
bluster, signifying nothing more than narrowness and vanity. He thought the liberal pulpit
rejected certain dogmas about Christ, because
it wanted Christ himself brought nearer to us—
with the demand which he knew would plague
him with an unsatisfied passion to be more
like Him. He imagined that liberals were dis-

contented with the dogmas of atonement and salvation because they were against an easy gospel—that is, they were willing to stand naked before the Awful Holiness, seeking "purity rather than peace," as Newman made his motto.   In short, if he was anxious for religion to be liberal, he was far more concerned that liberalism should be religious in a radical, creative, deep-going fashion, issuing in heroic moral action.   As a result he found himself an orthodox heretic among liberals and a liberal heretic among the orthodox; and that is where he stands today.

No matter; it is far more important to understand Dr. Orchard and his message than it is to try to classify him in one category or another, much less to paste a label on his cassock.   At the King's Weigh House in London, as in his earlier ministry in Enfield, he attracts an eclectic audience from all over the city, drawn equally by his shattering criticisms of the older views of theology and the positive message which no utterance of his ever lacks— but still more by a grace of personality and an authentic spiritual genius which mark him as a God-illumined preacher.   Not a few insist

that the rarest power of Dr. Orchard is his
gift of prayer, as revealed in his golden little
book, *The Temple,* which has done so much
to help men of the modern mind to walk once
more the quiet way to the Place of Hearing. Brief, tender, wistful, heart-probing, its
prayers are like those paving stones one finds
in unexpected places on the Yorkshire moors,
marking a broken and half-forgotten path over
the heather toward an ancient shrine of faith,
Whitby Abbey, uplifted on its stately headland
above the northern sea. It is a modern devotional classic, the like of which it would be hard
to name, unless it be *Spoken Words of Prayer
and Praise,* by Tipple, whose prayers are
lyrics of the love of God and the beauty of his
world, sun-bright and attuned to the songs of
birds, albeit not lacking in sympathy for the
struggle and tragedy of life. In my London
Diary I find the following memory of my first
service at the King's Weigh House, the Sunday
evening before I returned to my work at the
City Temple in 1917:

May 12th:—Went to King's Weigh House
Church today—made famous by Dr. Binney—
and heard W. E. Orchard preach. He is an

extraordinary preacher, of vital mind, of authentic insight, of challenging personality. From an advanced liberal position he has swung toward the Free Catholicism, and by an elaborate use of symbols is seeking to lead men by the sacramental approach to the mystical experience and the social expression of religion.   Some attend for the service, some for the sermon, and together they make an influential following.   The sermon had to do with the vision of Isaiah in the temple—a favorite theme in these days when so many things are shaken—and seldom have I heard a preacher more searching, more aglow with the divine passion.   He does not simply kindle the imagination; he gives one a vivid sense of reality.   He has a dangerous gift of humour, which sometimes sharpens into satire, but he uses it as a whip of cords to drive sham and unreality out of the temple.   He said that preaching in our day is bad, and that in the Anglican church "it is really worse than necessary!"   Much ado is now made about reordination, and he thought that it is not enough for the bishop to lay his hands on a preacher; the servant-girl and the tram-driver ought also to add their consecration.   With the lift of God in his face he cried: "You need Christ, and I can give him to you!"   Surely that is the ultimate grace and glory of the pulpit—the living Christ mediated to men.   It recalled the oft repeated record in the *Journal* of Wesley, in respect of the companies to whom he preached: "I gave them Christ." It was more than an offer; it was a sacrament of communication.

Such an entry gives no details of the picture, no account of the service with its strange blend of mediævalism and modernity, no description of the man who is the most impelling preacher in London, as he is often the most perplexing and irritating. A tiny wisp of a man, with tow hair and searching blue eyes, if in the pulpit he looks like an ascetic, in private he is the most joyous of comrades and the best story teller in England. At first the service, with its quick changes of artistic vestments, suggests a kindergarten parade of ecclesiastical millinery—in which Leviticus is substituted for Galatians, and the crucifix for the cross—until one has read his remarkable sermon on "Colour in Religion," and knows what he means by it. Behind him in the pulpit hangs a crucifix, and he often seems to appeal to it beseeching the Master to speak through him the living word. For sheer intellectual power, for keenness of spiritual insight—its authority marred, at times, by priestly assumption—he is as unique in his appeal as he is inimitable in his oratory. His brilliant asides, swift and sharp as a rapier-thrust, with enough slang in them to make them spicy, would not survive revision in print, but they are tellingly effective. When, however, we get beyond his humour, his satire, his gadfly criticism—which entitle him to be called the Bernard Shaw of Nonconformity— we find ourselves face to face with something that grips and pierces, and will not let us go. It is not of the intellect merely; it is a passion for souls which softens the sharpest edges of his thought and irradiates even his most cutting sarcasm. As another has written with true insight:

At the heart of his theology is a Christ who, feeling the urgency of the divine will upon him, and yielding himself up with the utmost single- ness of purpose and the most complete self- abandonment to the impulse of Saviourhood latent in every man, obtained that "Name that is above every name," whereby all men must be saved. Suddenly a note of passion creeps into the clear, sympathetic voice, bringing us up against something really great and search- ing, and all the minor irritations are forgot- ten. Suddenly the preacher grips reality with naked hands and all side issues sink below the surface. He is speaking of the reality of the

soul, of sin, of the human will, of God, of
Christ. Terrible in some moods is his unspar-
ing surrender to truth, his incorruptible attitude towards reality. He refuses to eat the
bread of compromise, spurns all cheap pragma-
tisms, scorns to debase religion into a mere
means of human happiness. He does not pal-
ter with the irony, the exactions, the crushing
sternness of the love of God; he does not trick
himself or others into believing that Jesus can
be loved with immunity. His Christ is the
Christ whose words fling fire on the earth,
whose touch leaves wounds, whose cross shat-
ters our little providential theories and tempts
us to cry out in our passionate hours that it is
a cruel and bitter thing to be loved of God.
Men who have so learnt Christ have a Herod-
sword within their hearts, and by an inalien-
able birthright belong to the spiritual aristocracy. If such a man is a preacher, especially
if he is a born preacher like Dr. Orchard, he
will fling fire among men and live to see it
kindle.[1]

From the first day of the Great War to the
last, Dr. Orchard stood in his pulpit and
pointed to the crucifix, at once a prophet of
indignation and a priest of pity. He preached
no interim ethics. If he was called a pacifist
it did not matter; he refused to lower the Chris-

[1] *Voices of Today,* by Hugh Sinclair.

tian ideal an inch.   Insistently, consistently,
with passionate and surrendering conviction
he bore magnificent and ceaseless witness
against all war.   His criticism was merciless, his sarcasm withering, and he spared no
one however high in office.   Through it all one
felt an infinite heartache, as of one who was
himself crucified by the agony of it all.   Re-
turning one day from Scotland, in a railway
carriage, I heard one British officer say to
another: "I say, old chap, it's a beastly business, this war.   It tears me in two.   Over here
we sing Peace on Earth, and out there the kill-
ing of boys goes on.   When I get so fed up I
can't stand it any longer, I go to a little chapel
in Duke Street, where a chap named Orchard
blows the whole blooming business up.   All I
can do is to swear, but he gets it said.   It's rip-
ping to hear him do it."   Had Dr. Orchard
exercised such a ministry in New York, no
doubt he would have landed in jail, so much
greater is the freedom enjoyed in England.
In my diary are a number of entries about him
and I venture to transcribe another:

May 10th, 1918:—What the Free Catholicism may turn out to be remains to be disclosed:

so far it is more clever and critical than constructive. W. E. Orchard is its Bernard Shaw, and W. G. Peck its Chesterton. At first it was thought to be only a protest against the ungracious barrenness of Nonconformist worship, in behalf of rhythm, colour, and symbolism. But it is more than that. It seeks to unite personal religious experience with its corporate and symbolical expression, thus joining two things hitherto held apart. As between Anglicans and Nonconformists it discovers the higher unity of things which do not differ, and that is a distinct advance. For, if we are ever to have Christian union, it must be by comprehension, not by compromise. It ought to be possible for those who emphasize individual experience of religious reality to unite with those who seek the corporate fellowship of believers. Together they may approach the largeness of Christ, in whom there is room for every type of experience and expression. Also, by interpreting and extending the sacramental principle, and at the same time disinfecting it of magic and superstition, the Free Catholicism may give new sanction and inspiration to creative social endeavour. For years it has been observed how many ultra High Churchmen—for example, Bishop Gore, one of the noblest characters in modern Christianity—have been leaders in the social interpretation and application of Christianity. Perhaps, at last, we shall learn that it was not the church, but humanity, with which Jesus identified himself when he said, "This is my body broken for you." There is still further light to break forth from Christian truth, and let us hope that the Free Catholicism will help us to see and follow it. The great thing about Christianity is that no one can tell what it will do next.

Perhaps this entry may help some of those who misunderstand Dr. Orchard to see the kind of Catholicism of which he is a prophet and a pioneer. Some imagine that by Catholicism he means the Roman Church, but that is neither free nor catholic. No one knows better than Dr. Orchard that Rome, as it now is, would crush him as quickly, as contemptuously, as she did Tyrrell, and with a tragedy far more ghastly than that of Newman. For while he has much that reminds one of Newman, he is a free spirit, and he knows the way to Emmaus as Newman never did. Others think that his Catholicism is merely æsthetic and temperamental, a sentimental attachment to some antique survival, like a fondness for Gothic architecture or a new version of the Mass. Far from it. He would, no doubt, restore much, if not all, of the old Catholic system, but without the spirit of anathema, exclusion, and compulsion,

676266

uniting the cultus of Christianity with its creed, and interpreting both in terms of eternal truth and modern need. Thus his vision is far wider, more comprehensive, more revolutionary than his critics are aware. Recently he said: "Some of you have been reassured about me lately that I am not going over to Rome, after all. I am not so sure. I may! But why are you not afraid that I may join the Salvation Army? Because equally I may! What I hate are the middle ways."

No; the Free Catholicism is far more catholic than the Roman Church, and it is freer than the Free Churches. It is a rediscovery of the comprehensiveness of Christianity, a living experience of the universality of Christ, as much at home with the Inner Light of the Quaker as with the Real Presence. But it joins depth with breadth, and finds in the old Christian dogmas not metaphysical abstractions, but dynamic forces for the creation of new men and a new social order, linking mystical vision with social passion, and freedom with fellowship. One has only to read the sermons of Dr. Orchard, who follows the old elaborate homiletic method—what the English call "the three-deck sermon"—to discover how profoundly radical the Free Catholicism is both as to personal experience and social regeneration. For the two are inseparable in his thought, as witness such sermons as "How the Cross Reconstructs Personality," and "Christian Dogma and Social Revolution." Here is vital preaching, as ancient as it is modern, aglow with insight and passion and prophecy; the voice of one who has the genius of a pathfinder, and the courage to make experiments, knowing that as of old Jesus "made as though he would have gone further," so, today, he beckons us toward his own largeness. In a striking sermon entitled "The New Catholicism," he says:

This then is the New Catholicism. At present it is no more than a dream in the hearts of a few, rather misty and vague perhaps, yet able to make every waking hour full of unrest for its realisation. With others it is only a dumb craving for they know not what, a discontent with things as they are. It has yet to outline its policy and fight its battles; and before it can conquer, there are prejudices to overcome, fears to dispel, false conclusions to disprove. Yet it holds the field. Denominationalism can no longer count upon the old-time loyalties. Neither Protestantism nor Romanism can ever do anything but stand over against one another, hostile and suspicious. There can be no reconciliation until they are gathered into one really Catholic Church. . . . Such hopes can only be realised as we get back to the catholicity of Christ's character and teaching. It is following names instead of Christ that has ruined us all. It is the attempt to employ worldly power instead of the wisdom of the Cross. It is a false scholarship that has given us a divided Christ. Only as we discover the One Catholic Christ shall we be able to build the One Catholic Church.

If in this appreciation the emphasis has been laid as much upon the message as upon the messenger, it is because the Minister of the King's Weigh House stands before us a shining and challenging figure, at once a rebuke and a portent. With the spiritual radicalism of his Master, he puts to scorn our comfortable conventionalism, our plausible expediences, our Pickwickian endeavours after Christian unity, no less than our compromising cowardice in the presence of the organised brutality of modern industrial and political life. When one thinks of the tragedy of a divided, distracted, ineffective church—a mere huddle of sects, each clinging to its own little dialect—set over against the federated iniquity of the world, one thanks God for a prophet-priest like Dr. Orchard; as much for his teasing humour, his tormenting satire, and his tantalising waspish criticism, as for his radiant insight and eloquence. Let him wear his gorgeous vestments and use the ancient symbols and litanies of faith, if by any means he can help to bring back the visions that make the church the sacramental incarnation of Christ. Frail, fearless, fascinating, across the tumbling seas I can still see him as he stood at his high altar, having poured out his heart in protest against the collective suicide of war, making the gesture of the Cross in benediction—as if to point us, in parable as well as precept, to the living Christ whose anointed messenger he is.

VI: Charles D. Williams

Can a prophet be a bishop? Can a bishop be a prophet? What is the function of a radical democrat in an old, aristocratic institution? What is the prophetic message for the ministry of today? Such questions were in my mind as I mingled with the divinity students at Yale when Bishop Williams gave his first lecture on preaching on the Lyman Beecher Foundation. It was an eager, expectant company, and some seemed waiting to see a long-haired, wild-eyed radical whose sentences would be a series of explosions. The lecturer, except for his clerical garb, looked more like a clear-cut, straight-seeing business man than a prophet of any kind; but behind his quiet manner and simple style one felt the glow of a divine fire. The genuineness of the man, his earnestness, his courage, his intellectual honesty, his spiritual passion won the day. The title of the course, "The Prophetic Ministry for Today," was characteristic of a teacher to whom religion is a vision, but a vision to be worked out practically in business, politics, industry, and legislation, no less than in the lonely conflicts of the inner life.

Unfortunately, I was able to hear only the first lecture in the course, which was a composite portrait of the Christian ministry—a series of dissolving views in which the Hebrew prophet, the Hebrew priest, the apostolic administrator, and the Greek sophist or rhetorician were blended. As in every such photograph, one saw when he had finished dim traces of each type; but it was clear that the lecturer thought the prophet faith and spirit ought to be supreme. The priest, the executive, and especially the rhetorician, ought to be subordinate, a point which he emphasised with some rather sharp words about flowery eloquence.

Howbeit, no man can be a prophet fifty-two days in the year, no matter how brightly the fire burns. There are interludes of teaching and administration—what St. Paul called "helps and governments"—which often make passages of prose in the poetry of the ministry. There is also the danger, he said, that the running of wheels may finally run to wheels, and a man meant to be a prophet ends by being the pastor of "The Church of the Holy Fuss," where the wheels go round but get nowhere. Once in the lecture he gave us a glimpse of the life of a bishop, which made all of us vow never to accept such an office—reminding one of the words of Bishop Gore when he resigned as Bishop of Oxford. In the preface to the volume in which the lectures now appear he makes the glimpse more vivid, confirming us in our resolution:

There is no motto more applicable to a modern Bishop than the text, "Gather up the fragments that nothing be lost." He is a man "scattered and peeled," troubled about many things, distracted with various and often mutually variant occupations. He must be a man of affairs and many affairs. He is expected to fulfil many functions. He is primarily a business man, an administrator and executive. Particularly he is the "trouble man" of a large corporation. All the "church quarrels" gather about his devoted head. He has the responsibility for everything that goes wrong, often without the authority to set anything right. He serves as a lightning rod to carry off the accumulated wrath of the ecclesiastical heavens. He is constantly called on to act as judge and should have a judicial temperament.

108 Some Living Masters of the Pulpit

He is also a "travelling man," a kind of ecclesiastical "drummer" or salesman. He is even
sometimes in demand as a social ornament to
say grace at banquets, make after-dinner
speeches, adorn the stage at public meetings,
and administer to the æsthetic needs of conventional society at fashionable weddings, bap-
tisms and funerals. In the midst of it all he is
expected to find time and mind to be a preacher
and teacher, a scholar and leader, and above
all a man of prayer and a man of God.

Two weeks later Bishop Williams preached
in the Cathedral of St. John the Divine—that
noble Home of the Soul slowly rising on the
cathedral heights of New York City, about
which James Lane Allen wove his lovely story,
The Cathedral Singer. While waiting for
the service to begin I found myself inquiring
in the sanctuary in respect to two matters
which weighed heavily upon my heart. What
is the function of the cathedral in a democracy? Can it give our tangled modern world
a common principle, a common passion, a common idea as it did the middle ages, when it
sent the common man in his multitudes away
to the crusades? Today we have no unifying
principle to hold the world together. The

nations seem to be drifting apart, and the classes in each are falling asunder, lacking a common ideal, a common faith, and a common hope. Would not a common form of worship —not so rigid as to become a mere rote or rigmarole, but with a common rhythm, at once corporate and communal, bringing art to the service of faith—do something to evoke a sense of common fellowship and obligation, and help to heal the appalling spiritual loneliness and chaos in which we find ourselves? In a cathedral all kinds and classes of people, learned and unlearned alike, are touched by a sense of mystery and awe which, if only for a brief time, brings each into the presence of a Reality which makes all one in their littleness and longing. In the midst of my reverie the organ began, but, like the writer of the 73rd Psalm, some solution of my problem seemed possible under that high and hospitable roof of God.

It was a notable occasion, made so by the daring of the preacher, whose sermon quickly shattered my mediæval mood, by showing how many clamorous questions from the noisy world intrude into the peace of a modern cathedral. The sermon provoked a heated discussion in the days following, as much for its rebuke of the hysteria and mob-mindedness of the moment when the Wilson-phobia was at its height, as for its castigation of certain reactionary influences seeking to capitalise an ugly mood for their own advantage. America was "seeing red," in a mood of mingled anger, hate and fear, actually having a cataleptic fit of terror at thought of a few radicals—like an elephant frightened at a mouse. It required some courage to speak plainly in face of such a mood, at a time when the pulpit seemed cowed and terrorised, and anyone who dared to dissent from the madness of the hour was branded as a bolshevist, a socialist, an anarchist, or some other thought-saving epithet. The bishop not only stood erect against the storm, but he spoke pointedly about the steel strike, the open-shop campaign, and the absurd intolerance of the moment. In particular, he denounced the "invisible government" of the privileged few which, he said, was seeking to control pulpit, as well as academic and legislative, utterances. At once there was an uproar, and *The Wall Street Journal* asked exasperatedly: "Was it the bolshevists or the business men who built and endowed the Cathedral of St. John the Divine?" The implication of such a question is that, since Big Business builds cathedrals, it has the right to dictate what is preached in their pulpits; and that is a fact worth knowing. The next Sunday the bishop-elect of New York preached in reply, deprecating the preaching of politics, as if a sermon in defence of the present order is not as much "political-preaching" as a sermon in criticism of it. The matter was taken up by the secular and religious press of the country, and both bishops got as many brick-bats as bouquets; but the issue was clearly drawn.

The bishop of Michigan thus stands before us as a man who provokes controversies, not only by virtue of the causes he champions, but also by the picturesque and pungent manner in which he states his message. He is indeed one of the outstanding and challenging figures of our American Christianity—manly, brotherly, democratic, fearless, sincere, utterly loyal to his Master and a lover of humanity—and if he receives many floggings at the hands of his critics, he is wise enough to adopt the philosophy of the old couplet:

> Sticks and stones will break my bones,
> But words will never hurt me.

Happily he has a keen sense of humour which serves as a shield against the slings and arrows of his enemies, the while it makes him a charming companion; as when, albeit a single-taxer himself, he describes how an orator of that sect fixes you with his glittering eye, until he has proved that his scheme is a panacea for all the ills that flesh is heir to, "even the measles"; or when, in an impish mood, he mimics the holy whine—what Dickens called "the Heavenly Father voice"—with which the curate intones the service. It does not matter that he is called a radical, a notoriety seeker, and an inciter of unrest; such things are a part of a prophet's reward. The chief fact about him is his profound earnestness, his fine sanity, and his vision of the religion of Jesus as practical fraternal righteousness. Yet even his friends have misgivings, at times, as to his methods, as witness these words of an able and high-minded journalist—words the more remarkable when we remember that any working journalist sees enough of the seamy side of humanity to equip half a dozen cynics:

As a preacher the bishop is earnest, forceful, intellectually honest, and tremendously courageous, and he marshals his facts well. Yet, somehow, I have always thought of him as a social, political and economic leader, rather than as a churchman. He has the two fisted belligerence of the worldly advocate, rather than those spiritual refinements we are supposed to associate with the pulpit. Yet he may be right, and our laymen's point of view all wrong, as to what a church leader should be. I do not know. He finds religion in the city streets and shops and factories; it is not something to be spiritualised and saved up for use only on Sundays. Whether his idea of the Christian church be right or wrong, he lives up to it; and because of his attitude he is beloved by the labouring men of the city, and is either feared, simply disliked, or blindly hated by that element in his church which pays its pew rent by the year and is eminently respectable—ah, yes, respectable though the heavens fall! Being a member of that church I know something of their quaint philosophy, and I really think that some of them would rather lose their souls than the world's respect.

Yet, when I hear the bishop in church, I always feel that I would rather hear him as a great leader of worldly affairs, on the floor of the United States Senate for example. Morally and intellectually he holds me tight, but I have heard other men who could stir me more deeply spiritually. Or should I say emotionally? No doubt this feeling is due to generations behind me who held, as my father used to say, that the Episcopal church is a good one to belong to, because it never interferes either with politics or religion. On politics, economic and social issues the bishop has always been consistently liberal, sane, and sensible—sane, of course, because he agrees with me. From time to time radicals have tried to tie him up with their extreme proposals, but he has always avoided them. Personally I think this is his field, unless, after all, it is conceded that this is the field of the church. Either the church, as it is now organised, has outgrown its usefulness and the bishop is a pioneer in a new order of Christianity, or the church is right and he is wrong. Certainly they do not hitch, at least in their philosophic outlook.

Some of us would rejoice to see the bishop of Michigan in the United States Senate—nowhere is spiritual vision more needed; but does not the church have need of a robust, forthright, statesman-like leadership? Surely, if

Christianity is to be more practical, more socially-minded, less sectarian and more creative, and not simply "a device to give peace of mind in the midst of conditions as they are," such leadership is the first necessity. In short, if Christianity be the realisation of God and the practice of brotherhood, then Bishop Williams is both a pioneer and a prophet. Those who say that he is not "spiritual" mistake emotional pietism for spirituality, as if truth, justice, and brotherhood were less spiritual than the rhythm of a ritual or the devoutness of Lent! The bishop holds that brotherhood—by which he means practical brotherhood, not a vague, dreamy sentiment—is not merely a poetic gesture in the Gospel of Jesus, but a fundamental principle; and that it is the mission of the church not only to redeem individuals, but also to help create an environment in which men can live the life of the spirit. He thinks the salvation of the church lies in its becoming once more the church of the lowly, since it is more important to have small churches of earnest men and women, poor but godly, than large churches housed in magnificent edifices—if it is necessary to temper the

Gospel to the rich in order to gain their support.

Hence the cry of socialist, anarchist, bol-shevist, and all the rest of the new vocabulary of profanity now in vogue, like jazz music. In olden times men threw stones at their prophets, but today they call names, finding abuse an easy substitute for the insight necessary to understand. The tragedy of our day is that we seem dead-locked between a narrow, selfish individualism on the one side and a visionary absurdity on the other, unable to find a fourth dimension. It so happens that Bishop Williams is not a Socialist at all, but a Christian teacher who finds in the gospel of Christ a way out of the dilemma. No one knows better than he that property, if honestly come by, represents moral values; and for that very reason it must be used in moral ways and for moral ends. It is not a question of the ownership of property, but of its moral and Christian use, modified by a sense of the common good, and, above all, by a sense of the sanctity of the human soul as the greatest and most precious of earthly realities. Therefore the bishop holds that Judge Gary has no right to cling to the twelve-

hour day in the steel mills, because it debases
and brutalises human souls, destroying that
holy thing which Christ came to seek and redeem.   So long as the lives of men, women,
and little children are ground up in the machinery of industry in order to make money,
he insists that the church must speak out
specifically, emphatically, insistently, and that
to be silent or neutral is to betray the Master.
In regard to these and other matters the bishop
has his own way of speaking out, which he
would hardly ask, expect, or encourage all his
clergy to follow; and no one can deny that it
is effective.   Some of his sayings are very
striking, and they hit the mark:

If the Lord in desperation—pardon the
phrase—should say, "I will feed these down-
trodden, starving children of mine," and rain
brown bread and molasses upon the earth, it
would do nothing to help the poverty of the
world under our present system.   It would
merely raise the value of the land where the
fall was heaviest.

We are soft and flabby because this is a day
of self-indulgence.   If a thing is agreeable, we
do it.   If it is disagreeable, we do not.   This
is the chief reason for the divorce problem.

Homes are wrecked, moral life is undermined, children are damned because "I was unhappy."

The habit of decision, of swift moral action is lost. In the business world, statutes are broken and moral laws are shattered, because "a man must get ahead." Any principle is sacrificed rather than make a failure, because a failure is unpleasant. We are devotees of the pleasant, the agreeable, the successful— the slaves of comfort. We are morally short of wind, worshippers of the god of ease; our moral discrimination is blurred.

My ancestry has been American for two hundred years; my family has fought in all the wars of the republic. I am not a bolshevik, parlor or otherwise. I am not a socialist, pink or white. As far as I can tell I am a plain, downright American. But I cannot stand this stage brand of 100 per cent Americanism that is up today. It is not Americanism. By the history of our nation, I call it Prussianism.

Our task is to make an imperfect Christian civilisation more Christian, but three kinds of impossibilists stand in the way. One is the blind individualist, the conventional Christian, who does not see the task at all. Another is the pessimist who resorts, as pessimists always do, to the apocalyptic and eschatological. He is the premillenarian. The third is the visionary idealist, the man with a panacea, with complete specifications of the heavenly city down to the last brick in the pavement.

There are lions in the way. There are difficulties and dangers and demands as you go
forth into our prophetic ministry, but these are
so many challenges and opportunities which
make it the most glorious day in which men
could be called to that ministry. Marcus Dodds
once said, "I do not envy those who have to
fight the battle of Christianity in the twentieth
century. Yes, perhaps, I do, but it will be a
stiff fight." And let me add, a stiff fight is
what the true soldier of Christ loves.

If in this study I have laid less emphasis
upon the teacher than upon his teaching, it is
because he incarnates, as much by his office
as by his insight, issues which will confront us
increasingly in the days that lie ahead. The
sum of his teaching, as well as the art which
he employs, may be found in a book of sermons
entitled, *A Valid Christianity for Today,*
which, by any test, must be reckoned as one of
the most virile and arresting volumes in the
literature of the American pulpit. Some of its
sermons—such as The Religion of Democracy,
Dives and Lazarus, and The Supreme Value—
are of enduring worth and power; they search
our hearts like flames of fire. The mysticism
of the book—for, as Phillips Brooks said, mys-

ticism is the heart of religion, without whose ever-beating life the hands of religion, which do the work, fall dead—is social as well as individual, and less contemplative than active. It is like the pity in the hearts of the medical students at Edinburgh, of which Dr. Brown wrote in a haunting passage; a pity, he said, which finds expression not in trembling tears and long-drawn sighs, but in clearer insight and a firmer and more skilful hand in healing the hurts of humanity. It is the vision of a man who sees that all life is sacramental, and that the Kingdom of God is a beloved community of noble men and women who do noble things together, making the service of man a ritual for the worship of God.

Even those who account themselves conservative—whether by nature or by grace—must surely thank God for the heroic ministry of Bishop Williams, both as prophet and statesman. If they do not always agree with his teaching or method, they ought to be ready to fight for his right to teach the truth as God gives him to see it with every art at his command—a right now challenged in his own communion—in behalf of a complete and comprehensive Christian witness in a sorely baffled world. St. James did not preach like St. John, nor did St. Peter and St. Paul always agree— each finding in the other things hard to understand—but together, by a fraternity of insight and experience, they expounded a profound and many-sided gospel, which, at last, will win all our various and imperfect tones into one sovereign harmony. This lesson is for us, reminding us that the Gospel of Jesus is deeper, richer and larger than our individual insight and emphasis; and, further, that though we have the eloquence of an angel and the zeal of a martyr, and have not brotherly love, we are as dead. God be thanked for a prophet-bishop! Long may he labour among us!

VII: A. Maude Royden

The story of how the greatest woman preacher of our generation was discovered and pushed into the pulpit, is after this manner. As had been anticipated both by myself and by the officers of the City Temple, it soon became plain that I must have a colleague in my work. Indeed, it had been so agreed before I landed in England, and as a condition of my acceptance of the Temple ministry. The strain of three sermons each week, with so many outside demands, had taxed the strength of a giant like Dr. Parker—who often enough "warmed over" old material on a Thursday—and it had nearly killed R. J. Campbell. Besides, invitations were pouring in upon me from all over the kingdom, and the City Temple people sympathised entirely with my plan for a larger ministry of interpretation between the two countries. But to find a colleague was no easy undertaking—so many preachers were

already at the war that churches had to
double up.

Since England was at that time a world of
women, and woman was entering upon a life
new and strange and difficult, it seemed to some
of us that if a great woman of genius could be
found the problem would be solved. Such a
thing could not have been done before the
war without a hubbub of criticism, and it would
have been denounced as a Yankee innovation.
But the war had changed everything. Woman
had been in revolt; now she was triumphant,
the vote, about which there had been so much
bother, having become a mere bagatelle to be
taken for granted. She had shown her worth
in the war, taking the place of man even in
hard, heavy work. There was need of a woman of vision to interpret the new life of woman,
its spiritual meaning no less than its obligations and aspirations, if only the right one
could be found to meet the need.

Of women preachers there had been a few
in England before, and many in America—
from the days of Mary Livermore down—but
on neither side of the Atlantic had any woman
ever been chosen as a regular assistant in a

great city pulpit. Fearsome things were prophesied of so revolutionary an arrangement; even a few of the City Temple folk hesitated, much depending, as they said, upon the woman selected. Fortunately we found in Miss A. Maude Royden the woman exactly fitted by genius, by training, by temperament, and by courage to attempt a great work and do it. Yet, as a fact, though devout almost to asceticism, she had never tried to preach, and apparently had not thought of doing so, knowing, as a loyal daughter of the Church of England, that she would not be allowed to preach in her own communion. She did not know whether she could preach or not. Nor did we. Finally, not without misgiving and much persuasion, she agreed to try, and, as all now know, the attempt was brilliantly vindicated. The secular press welcomed the innovation with enthusiasm, and even the religious papers —with exceptions, of course, chiefly among the Anglican journals—accepted it as an inevitable "sign of the times," watching the experiment with interest and concern.

Sunday after Sunday large congregations gathered to hear Miss Royden, some drawn

by curiosity at first, but all remained to pray;
and if the majority of her audiences were
women, it was to be noted that many men
in khaki found her preaching a blessing.
Naturally, in private, I had to bear the brunt
of criticism, in a flood of letters sometimes
angry, and often ugly. Of course the words
of St. Paul about women keeping silence in
church were worn threadbare—so few knew
what he meant—and the gibe of Dr. Johnson
about a woman preaching being like a dog trying to walk on his hind legs, was not forgotten.
More than one letter reminded me of the dic-
tum of Montaigne that "women are hardly fit
to treat on matters of theology"; and so it
went, with much ridicule of "petticoats in the
pulpit." One Anglican layman did, however,
modify the saying of Henry Sidgwick for my
benefit: "Of course, it's nonsense, but it's
the right kind of nonsense." As often as I
met the Bishop of London, his chief concerns
seemed to be whether Miss Royden actually
stood in the pulpit of the City Temple, and
whether or not she wore a hat! It did not
matter; I was content to let facts refute folly,

and Miss Royden soon made her place in what proved to be her rightful sphere.

The daughter of Sir Thomas Royden, Bart., formerly Lord Mayor of Liverpool, in a home at once high church and ultra Tory, Miss Royden was born to a life of wealth, luxury, and culture. Like Beatrice she might have said, "Then there was a star danced and under it I was born"; but it was a pilgrim star making her a pioneer, a radical, a reformer, a leader of unpopular causes. Unlike Beatrice, she did not feel the sadness of the world only when she was asleep; the more awake she was the more she felt it, though never in a way to becloud a spirit to whom joy was native, beauty a sacrament, and life an adventure and a challenge. She was educated at Cheltenham College, going later into residence at Lady Margaret Hall, Oxford, where she took honours in modern history. After some work done in the slums of Liverpool and in a midland country parish, she became the first woman lecturer under the Oxford University Extension scheme, her subjects being history and literature. Always her interest lay less with the classes than with the masses, where, as Dostoevsky, her favourite novelist, had shown, so much of divinity is to be found.

For some years Miss Royden devoted herself to the cause of the enfranchisement of women, and as editor of *The Common Cause,* she very soon won a place of leadership in the law-abiding suffrage movement. To a smaller public she was known as an original thinker, an expert in all matters relating to the life of woman and child—having much the same position in England that Miss Jane Addams has long held in America—and a writer in behalf of a new internationalism. Indeed, she was a pleader for all great human causes, but especially for a purer social life, based, not upon legalisms, but upon a higher standard, equal for men and women, in morals, health, and culture. Yet, during all those labours and agitations, she kept an inviolate altar in her heart—true to the church in spite of its laggard and reluctant interest in prophetic human enterprises—uniting the devotion of a saint with a flaming social passion, and keeping both in poise by a dauntless faith, a calm reasonableness, and a rich and sparkling humour.

Slight of figure, frail unspeakably, with a

limp in her gait, as an orator Miss Royden is
unique in her simplicity—direct, forthright,
winsome. She reminds me more of Frances
Willard—"St. Frances, of Evanston," as I love
to call her—than anyone I remember to have
heard, albeit with more verve and fire. Rich,
mellow, unfaltering, her voice is singularly revealing, her articulation perfect, and, without
a trace of sentimentality, she speaks to the
heart. There is no shrillness in her eloquence,
no impression of strain, no affectation. She
speaks with the exquisite ease of long practice,
in a style more conversational than oratorical,
and is more at home in an assembly where the
people can answer back, whether on a chair at
the street corner, or at a conference of a band
of rescue workers, or wherever the common
people foregather.

At first she was not at home in the pulpit of
the City Temple, until she started an after
meeting in which her hearers could have their
say, discussing questions suggested by the
sermon, or the problems of the religious life.
Some of her epigrams are unforgettable in
their quick-sighted summing up of situations,
as when she said in the Royal Albert Hall, to

the horror of deans and bishops: "The church of England is the conservative party at prayer." One secret of her influence and power may be found in the faith thus confessed: "I am convinced that what I can see others can see, and nothing will persuade me that the world is not ready for an ideal for which I am ready." Untrained in theology—which some hold to be an advantage—she deals with the old issues of faith as an educated, spiritually-minded woman in sensitive contact with life, inspired by a lofty faith and guided by a sanctified common sense worth more than much dogma. She casts aside the "muffled Christianity" which Wells once described as the religion of the well-to-do classes, holding resignation to be "a detestable virtue," however canonical, if it means that worship is to be an opiate and the sermon a dose of soothing syrup. Not only stimulating but provocative—seldom provoking—it is no wonder that she shocked many of the staid, unco-respectable folk when she made her advent in the City Temple.

Nothing was plainer than that the best way for me to help Miss Royden was to let her be entirely free; and I did so. Usually we had a conference once a month, or more often in case of emergency, and we never had but one difference of judgment—regarding sending a petition from the City Temple to the British government to lift the blockade, which, as an American citizen, I could not do, though I assured her she was free to denounce the blockade as she liked. Not the least important feature of the work of Miss Royden at the Temple, aside from the three services a month which she conducted, was what I called her "clinic"; that is, two or three days a week when she was in attendance at the City Temple, acting as guide, confidant and friend to hundreds of women, and as priest and confessor to not a few. Here she did what no man born may ever hope to do. Woman can comfort and counsel woman in a way unique. Tactful, large souled, wisely sympathetic, she entered deeply into the problems of those who consulted her, gaining a clear insight into the real needs of the modern soul astray in its own life—wistful, lonely, troubled, longing for an experimental sense of spiritual reality, yet only half willing to submit to the discipline of the quest. It meant much to young women bewildered by perplexity, or broken by bereavement, to meet and take counsel with a woman like Miss Royden. And this ministry of conference and confession reacted, in turn, upon her preaching, making it peculiarly effective in meeting the issues, both spiritual and social, confronting present day womanhood.

There was a brief outcry of criticism when Miss Royden christened a child one Sunday—a service performed with such grace and impressiveness that it was not soon forgotten— but the critics were soon hushed. Personally I should have been glad to have had her administer the Lord's Supper, but she thought it best not to do so, lest it expose her to rebuke, if not to discipline, by the authorities of the Anglican church, to which she remained loyal, and some of whose leaders resented her ministry in the City Temple. Indeed, the Bishop of London actually inhibited her from conducting a Good Friday service in one of the city churches under his obedience, to the horror of multitudes of Christian people who felt that on that day, of all days, no voice of prayer should be hushed. It seemed to many that the Bishop—whose foresight is not abnormal—had

been wiser, if, instead of driving Miss Royden
out of the church, to consort with feminists,
intellectuals and social revolutionaries, he had
set her the task of bringing them inside. But
apparently he was more concerned about her
hat than about what she was doing with the
brains under her hat! Like John Wesley, she
may remain all her days in the Anglican fold,
but she will be there only in her private
capacity, and her influence will be centrifugal.

At any rate, I gave a great woman a great
opportunity, to which she measured up, vindi-
cating once for all the possibilities of a woman
of genius in the service of the Christian pulpit;
and together we gave an example of that Christian unity of which we heard so much and saw
so little. In short, the woman insight, the
woman touch, the woman point of view were
needed in the pulpit, as elsewhere, and her
presence added to the City Temple ministry
a hint of that beautiful thing which we feel in
the Gospel of St. Luke. It was an honour to
have a colleague so gifted and so gracious, and
our fellowship was the more completely har-
monious, no doubt, because each could do what
the other could not do. As the war went on,

bringing a still further degradation of morals
in respect to the relations of the sexes—an
appalling letting down of the bars to the brute
—more than one issue came up with which
Miss Royden could deal in a manner impossible
to any man. She showed how a woman of
ethereal refinement and spirituality, while
speaking plainly, can handle such delicate and
difficult subjects as no man can handle them.
An entry in my London Diary speaks for
itself:

April 15, 1918:—When the question came
up as to the *Maison-Tolerees*—that is, houses
within the bounds of the British Army in which
women were herded, under medical super-
vision, for the uses of the soldiery—I had a
conference with Miss Royden, telling her that
the problem was hers. She agreed, and the
manner in which she has dealt with it is magnificent. Delicately, yet plainly, disguising
none of the beastliness of it, she stated the
case, and I have never seen such flaming wrath
of outraged womanhood against the degradation of her sex! To those who defended the
system—and I heard it defended in a group
of Christian ministers!—after describing the
tolerated house at Cayeux-sur-Mer, and denouncing the Government as a procurer in the
practise of prostitution, she said: "To any

woman who believes the sacrifice to be necessary, I would say that she ought herself to
volunteer! The men who urge regulated
prostitution on grounds of national necessity,
ought to invite their wives and daughters to
fill the places left vacant by the women who
are worn out! I use words that sear my heart,
but as a woman in a Christian pulpit I cannot
be silent in the presence of such an infamy!"
Soon the Government began to wince under
her attacks, and the abomination was abolished.
Unfortunately the Archbishop did not get
angry until after the victory had been won—
then he denounced the horror in the House of
Lords!

The ministry of Miss Royden at the City
Temple—memorable in many ways—ended
with my own, because she did not wish to em-
barrass my successor, and she feared that no
British minister would work with her as I had
done. In this she was happily mistaken. Later,
she and Dr. Dearmer, of King's College, held
services in the Kensington Town Hall with
conspicuous success—he speaking in the after-
noons, she in the evenings, to the vast audience
which follows her wherever she goes. For a
time she was a wanderer, a preacher to whom
no church would open its doors—a strange

situation at a time when so many churches,
both Anglican and Free, were empty! Finally
an abandoned church was secured, and she
and Dr. Dearmer have formed a Fellowship,
to which many restless, forward-looking
people are attracted—but, alas, ill health adds
a handicap to one already frail. Whatever may
be the future of Miss Royden, it was the City
Temple that discovered her and gave her an
opportunity equal to her powers. There, in a
setting and service often described—never
more vividly than by Archibald Marshall in
his story, *The Greatest of These*—the dark
little woman in the big white pulpit seemed in
accord with the fitness of things; and her
genius shone as a light of God in the cruel days
of war, and the still more cruel days of rancour
and reaction which followed.

VIII: Samuel McChord Crothers

A Nevada minister once described to me the action of a brother minister in the early days. The minister went to a certain town where he offended the lawless element, and was threatened with physical violence if he persisted in his intention of preaching. My friend described the method by which the liberty of prophesying was asserted. "He went into the pulpit, laid his revolver on the Bible—and then preached *ex tempore.*"

The manner of narration savoured of the soil. The Honest Miner under the circumstances would subordinate everything to emphasis on the correct homiletical method. No matter how able the minister might be, it was evident that if he were closely confined to his notes, his delivery could not be effective.

These words from an inimitable essay, "A Community of Humourists," [1] show us the difference between the humour of the backwoodsman and that of the miner of the west—

[1] *The Pardoner's Wallet.*

whither Dr. Crothers went from Union Seminary, driven by an illness which required the
high, clear air of the mountains. The humour
of the pioneer consisted in a grave, grotesque
exaggeration, while that of the miner is a delicate, deliberate understatement, like the con-
siderate notice posted by the side of an open
shaft: "Gentlemen will please not fall down
this shaft, for there are men at work below."
But the passage has a further significance more
pertinent to the matter in hand. As a fact, so
I have been told, it was after some such fashion
—happily without a threat of violence or the
need of a revolver—that Dr. Crothers himself
learned that he could preach without manuscript or notes; a discovery which added a
whole dimension to his power as a preacher.

The story, as it was told me on good authority, ran somewhat after this manner. It was
the first Sunday the young theologue ever appeared in a pulpit, and, supposing that he was
to have but one service on that day, he prepared only one sermon. The sermon was carefully written and apparently got itself preached
without mishap; but to his amazement, during
the morning service he was asked to announce

a second service in the evening at which he was to be the preacher. As the afternoon was taken up with engagements, and he had no time to prepare, he was obliged to preach off-hand, so to speak; and he did it with such ease and joy that he has never used manuscript since. It was a fortunate circumstance, and one often wishes that something of the sort might happen—as in the case of the prophet of Nevada, who dared not take his eyes off his audience lest he be shot—compelling all preachers to speak freely, frankly, and directly concerning the things that matter most.

The passage quoted above has a still further significance, as showing the wide experience Dr. Crothers has had of America, and especially of the west, which he has interpreted with so much insight and understanding. If asked where the west begins, he would answer that it begins "at that point where the centre of interest suddenly shifts from the day before yesterday to the day after tomorrow." No one knows America, he insists, until he has been touched by the fever of the west; and one who has felt that fever never completely recovers, but is always subject to intermittent

attacks.   Indeed, his life in Nevada and his
ministry in Minnesota qualify him to write
that psychological-geography of "The Land of
the Large and Charitable Air," which he suggests in an essay of that title.   Hence a chapter
on "The Lure of the West" in the best book
ever written in interpretation of Emerson [2] —
the best in its appreciative discrimination, and
because it treats the Sage of Concord not as
an oracle, but as a comrade and "con-
temporary"—who did "more than any one else
to redeem the New England group of authors
from the kind of provincialism which was their
darling sin."   Like Emerson, he knows the
robust, prophetic idealism of the west, and
loves it the more because it is still pushing its
way up through the hearty, wholesome ma-
terialism of a new country; and so long as
America keeps these two things together, it
will not go far astray.

Such is the background of the ministry of
Dr. Crothers to one of the most thoughtful
and cultured congregations in New England, in
the old First Parish of Cambridge—where not
a little of the old provincialism which Emerson

[2] *Emerson, How to Know Him.*

sought to correct is still to be found. There, in a church mellow with history, in a setting exquisite in its simplicity—colonial in aspect and arrangement—I heard Dr. Crothers preach not far from twenty years gone by. The atmosphere and impression of that hour are still vivid in my heart, and still more the radiant and benignant personality of the preacher—his grave, quiet manner, his deliberate delivery, his chaste and limpid style, his sly humour, his lofty and logical thought. At this distance I do not recall the text, but his theme was "Three Ancient Types of Religion," the priest, the prophet, and the philosopher; and he seemed to me to be a compound of all three. It so happened that I was in the first glow and enthusiasm of my discovery of Emerson, and I felt as King Herod must have felt when he heard of the preaching of Jesus, and thought he was John the Baptist returned from the dead. Indeed, all through the sermon I felt almost as if I were listening to Emerson— not that Dr. Crothers was an echo of the sage, or even a disciple, but he had the same wise and serene elevation of thought. So much was this true that I have hesitated to describe the impression of that day, fearing that the two men were blended, if not blurred, in my mind, like a dissolving view. But since reading his book on Emerson—in which we see how much the two have in common, and in what ways they differ—I am not sure that I was so far wrong, after all; and my faith is confirmed by a letter from a great and wise man who has attended the First Parish church for many years:

The study of Dr. Crothers as a preacher presents an interesting problem; for, in the ordinary sense of the word, he is not a preacher. He uses no hortatory eloquence, or application of his theme; nothing of the "Finally, my brethren," or "O my dear friends." He simply delivers himself of a thought, and lets it have its own way. In the details of parish affairs he is very childlike, and the simplest notice is a stumbling block to him. He is but slightly interested in the enrichment of worship, or its technical details. On the other hand, when he passes to the development of his thought, he is the finest master of logical and convincing speech I ever knew. With no shred of manuscript, and no appearance of effort, his sermon advances up the heights of insight and power with extraordinary continuity and force. In other words, he is at his

best when his thought is most elevated, and
least effective when dealing with ordinary
affairs. He is the lineal descendant of Emerson in the pulpit, directing a transparent
stream of purifying thoughtfulness. Such a
method removes him altogether from the position of a model for other preachers. An earlier
generation of Unitarian ministers ran much
risk of being spoiled by using a method which
is described as "Emerson and water." To
imitate Crothers without his genius for lucidity
would be a hopeless task. He is as much alone
in the pulpit as Emerson is in literature. The
consequences of this kind of ministry are, however, instructive. It is generally recognised
in his parish that he cannot be depended upon
as a mechanic or organiser. Accepting his inspiration, others do the work of organisation,
and his church has become distinguished for its
multifarious undertakings of social service. In
other words, the wheels go round because there
is a quietly moving and powerful engine among
them, like the Living Creatures among the
wheels, whom Ezekiel saw.

Unfortunately, for the purposes of this
article, Dr. Crothers is more widely known as
an essayist than as a preacher; and he can never
be really known as a preacher save by those
who hear him. His sermons, as we read them,
are essays—like most sermons in the Unitarian

ministry to which he belongs—that it might be fulfilled which was spoken by the prophet Emerson:

A new commandment, said the smiling Muse, I give my darling son, Thou shalt not preach.

But his essays are often sermons, and good ones, too, such as "The Cruelty of Good People," or the chapter in his study of Emerson entitled "Spent the Day at Essex Junction." A more helpful sermon than that chapter it would be hard to name, teaching us that we must learn how to find fulness of life everywhere, anywhere, even in "a place on the way to somewhere else." But the reason why one must hear Dr. Crothers in order to know him as a preacher is that his sermons are seldom, if ever, printed as they were delivered. Often there is as much humour in his preaching as in his essays, but the sermons are revised by him from the report of the stenographer, and he edits the humour out. This is matter for regret, not only because humour has a place in religion, but because the humour of Dr. Crothers is unique, blending the elusive smile of Emerson, the whimsical wisdom of Lamb, and the inverted exaggeration of the Honest Miner, with many ingredients all his own. Anyway, his printed sermons hardly give an adequate idea of the impression made upon his hearers. How he prepares his sermons some of us would like to know, just as we should like to know what use he makes, in these arid days, of a certain fund left to the First Parish by a benevolent saint of long ago, intended "to supply the minister with tobacco and rum." Of course, a man who has access to *The Pardoner's Wallet* enjoys obvious advantages; but the matter excites curiosity.

Almost thirty years have now come and gone since Dr. Crothers published his first volume of sermons, entitled *Members of One Body,* which happily may still be had. It was made up of a series of Sunday evening addresses during his ministry at St. Paul—when he was a kind of bishop of the northwest, starting new centres of liberal faith at Duluth, St. Cloud, and as far as Helena—dealing with the different types of the religious life, Catholicism, Calvinism, Methodism, Rationalism, Mysticism, and a final address on "The Unity of Christendom." Even in those early days he

was master of the same lucid style, and had
the same large outlook in which many apparently contradictory qualities were joined—
breadth and depth, rationalism and mysticism,
catholicity and missionary zeal, the wisdom of
a philosopher and the ardour of a reformer.
A more sincere appreciation of the great qualities of the Roman church it would be hard to
find; and so of the other types, his plea being
for men of the spirit who are co-operatively
minded, which requires them to get rid both of
narrowness and fastidiousness.   Toleration is
not enough; there must be insight, understanding, appreciation.   We must not simply live
and let live, think and let think; we must learn
that the devout life is everywhere the same,
"flowing underneath the thickest ice of theory,"
if we try to discern and understand.   What is
greater than any one of our sects?   All of
them! Our very recognition of the truth which
each contains should make us realise how
fragmentary each is.   As we may read:

When we assume this attitude, we begin to
see through all its variations of thought the
essential unity of Christianity.   The most opposite types have points of kinship.   Each of

them is aiming to get beyond sectarian narrowness, and to build a universal church. They agree as to their ideals: they disagree as to their way of reaching them. . . . How may this unity be practically realised? I have little hope in any external power that shall compel uniformity. I think such external union under present conditions neither desirable nor practicable. When we read that different competing firms have united their interests in one great trust, we expect very soon after to find a modest item in the papers to the effect that this trust has taken measures to limit production. And, were all the churches of Christendom united in one church, the next move would be to repress the liberty of prophesying. If we cannot have liberty and union, we must cling ever to liberty. But I am one who believes that through the most perfect liberty will come at last the most perfect unity.

There is no power in any sect or church that can prevent that largeness of sympathy which every man of true religion exercises. I like the good old New England puritan who, when he was excommunicated by the church, refused to stay excommunicated. We read that for twenty years the good man came every communion Sunday, and brought with him a bit of bread and bit of wine of his own, and there, in the safety of his high pew, communed with the church, in spite of the deacons. When a man brings his own communion with him, who can prevent? Whether we shall enjoy the communion of saints depends on ourselves. The best that belongs to Calvinism and the best that belongs to Romanism is mine, if I seek it. The fellowship of the spirit, which is the only fellowship that one need care to obtain—this fellowship is ours, if we will.

From heart to heart, from creed to creed,
The hidden river runs.

A second volume of sermons, entitled *The Understanding Heart,* appeared ten years later—he has published but two, though many of his sermons may be had in pamphlet form— yet one would not know that it is a volume of sermons at all. There are no texts to tell us so. There is none of the urgency or appeal that goes with preaching; no exhortation, no fervour of evangelism, such as we find in Theodore Parker. It is a book of essays for the elect, who know that the problems of the understanding heart are educational, and that only so can we readjust our thought and faith to the facts of a growing, but friendly, universe. How may our religious inheritance be harmonised with our fresh experiences? How may the institutions which have purely spiritual ends be adjusted to those which serve our ma-

terial welfare? How may we at the same time
live according to the rules of sound reason and
according to the inspirations of religious faith?
Such questions are discussed with fruitful insight, a gentle and revealing wisdom, and a
grace of form which marks all his work. The
readjustment must not be merely formal, but
must come through the multitudes of men and
women doing their work with joyous and confident intelligence, following the new develop-
ments as well as recording the old—organising
the religion of freedom, as of old men organised the religion of authority.

However, it is an error if I have left the
impression that Dr. Crothers lives aloft, writing exquisite essays in an ivory tower, aloof
from the interests and agitations of his age.
Not so. If to many he seems to live apart, his
very detachment gives him a clearer perspective, and more than once in his own communion
he has relieved the tension as much by his wisdom as by his humour. Some years ago when
John Haynes Holmes proposed, in a brilliant
speech, to commit the Unitarian church to a
definite programme of reform, it was Dr.
Crothers who made protest, not against reform,

but against tying the church to particular schemes. It was a picturesque occasion, and while he had to pay the penalty of being a man of humour, his triumph was due to sound sense. His protest was in behalf of freedom, and against any kind of coercion—whether by conservative or radical—and wisdom was on his side. First find your dogma, and then adapt yourself to it—such was the archaic method. It does not work theologically, and he did not believe it would work sociologically either. In other words, he did not want a new sectarianism for the old, but freedom in the largest, fullest sense—liberty of prophesying, and "the liberty of not believing more than half the prophet says." He said that if he had been in Jerusalem when Jeremiah proposed to let Nebuchadnezzar punish the nation as the scourge of God, he would have voted against him. The kind of prophets he likes are "prophets that have some sense, and a prophetic fervour behind"; as if any age ever regarded its prophets as sensible! In the same address he said:

A year or two ago a revivalist came to Boston preaching the new evangelism. The ministers met together and had daily meetings to stir the conscience of Boston, to bring again the old sense of sin. He was a good preacher. As a practical application of his preaching, the evangelist said to the business men who had come to the noonday meetings, "Let us go and march in a procession to find and save the sinners." Where do you think they went? They went up into the North End of Boston. A gentleman coming out of the meeting said to me, "That ends my interest in it: why did they not go on State street?" The ethical questions of today are like the ethical questions of the time when slavery was a source of revenue to good people. They go deep, sometimes they touch your interests and mine, and earnest men know that full well. Every attempt to found a church today on glittering generalities, where the preacher does not dare to follow to its practical and necessary issues the religion of the present generation, has no future: it has no interest for the young. . . . I believe these are great days, interesting days for the young men who are about to enter the ministry—men of clearness, of sagacity, of patience, of common sense, all mixed up with a great sense of humour. If they are patient enough and do not allow things to get too much on their nerves, they are going to win out.

Some think Dr. Crothers is at his best in his Harvard lecture on *The Endless Life,* if only because he has described once for all that of which—when the clouds are off our souls—we dare assert immortality. There he moves in a realm of moral and spiritual values, where his calm and clear insight shines like a friendly beacon. The future life, at once the polar expedition of philosophy and the polar star of faith, becomes in his hands a quest of the quality of life which reveals its own eternity. For him the final assurance is "the confidence of the simple man who stands in his integrity undaunted by death"; and while he does not profess to see "the lights o' Dover," he leaves us confident, but not curious—knowing that all is well because man brings down to the Gate of the Mist something that ought not to die.

IX: T. Reaveley Glover

In August, 1918, while waiting for a steamer to take me to America on a speaking tour, I heard six of a series of eight sermons by Dr. Glover at Westminster Chapel. He was preaching at the Chapel for a month, Dr. Jowett being away on a holiday, and the theme of his series dealt with "Jesus in the Experience of Men." Since that time he has written a book under the same title, as a sequel to his *Jesus of History;* but the sermons were different from the chapters of the book when it appeared. In some ways they were better than the book, one of them, for example, being in the form of a story, telling how the first statue of Jesus as the Good Shepherd was carved. They were not lectures, but preaching of a very real kind, at once stimulating and searching. It was interesting to study the congregations, many of whom were ministers —most of them on holiday, like myself—and all eager to hear Dr. Glover. It is always so,

whenever and wherever he speaks. In my diary
I find the following entry recalling those
summer days:

August 12, 1918:—Whether I get a steamer
or not does not much matter, so long as Dr.
Glover preaches at the Westminster Chapel.
His series of sermons on the Jesus of Experience will make as rich a book as his studies
of the *Jesus of History*. A layman who is a
Doctor of Divinity, an orator with an atrocious
elocution, he is a scholar who knows more than
the law allows any one man to know. At times
his manner suggests a professor in a class-
room, but he is a truly great preacher—simple,
direct, earnest, with no thought other than to
make clear his vision of Jesus in the lives of
men. Rarely have I heard sermons so packed
with forthright thinking and fruitful insight.
There is ripe scholarship without pedantry and
noble eloquence without oratory. Perhaps the
outstanding impression is a fresh, vivid sense
of reality, as of one who is looking straight at
the truth he is talking about. He "speaks
things," as Cromwell would say. Vital faith
and fearless thinking are joined with a conviction of the genuineness of the man, and his
knowledge of Jesus in his own experience. He
dodges no issue, no fact, no difficulty, and
his knowledge of the social, intellectual and
spiritual world in which Jesus lived, and in
which the church began her morning march,

is extraordinary. He has a curious power of taking us back into those times. There are many ministries, but one Spirit. Some are prophets, some evangelists, some teachers. Dr. Glover is a great teacher of the truth as it is in Jesus.

The first sermon of the series was preached on August 4th, the anniversary of that dark day, four years before, when England entered the war. Memories of that great decision, thoughts of its meaning, its cost in blood and sorrow, filled all our minds; and instead of the morning prayer Dr. Glover talked to us out of a full heart, in the gentle words which men use when they speak of such matters. What is the meaning of this "long-lived storm of great events?" he asked. What difference has it made? It is the task of the church, if it is to be the priest of God to the nation, to trace and measure the reactions of events in the deeper life of the people. How does it stand today in that inner life of thought, of motive, of faith, down where "the shell-burred cables creep?" The Bible, and especially the Old Testament, is a record of the reactions in the life of a nation to the terrible deeds of God.

The Assyrian army lives in the inner life of man, because through its movements the soul of Isaiah was given new reach and range of vision. When Titus destroyed Jerusalem he released into the world a new Israel, the church of Christ. Acts which absorb the minds of men at the moment live afterwards chiefly in the literature of the soul. Will it be so today? Surely he who awakened the soul of Israel through the march of the Assyrian host, has some word to speak in this terror and tumult. Who will read for us the new and living Word of God, written in the facts and events of the day? Are there elect souls who can hear for others the still small voice speaking in the storm? Then he asked all to join in the Lord's Prayer, as alone adequate to upbear the thoughts and yearnings of the hour. Never have I heard that brief, grand prayer so surcharged with feeling, lifting a troubled people into the fellowship and consolation of God.

The sermon which followed had two texts— 1 Cor. 2:8, and Heb. 8:8—portraying Christ the same yesterday, today and forever, in contrast with the phantasmagoria of "world-rulers of the darkness" which haunted the

ancient world. In *Paradise Lost* we see
that dæmon world, "thrones, dominions, prin-
cipalities and powers," in its most glorious
form, but we do not realise how real and
terrifying it was to the ancient mind. To us
all that history of war in the spirit sphere is a
dim, shadowy mythology, but to the men of
that day it was real, proven by long belief, and
confirmed by the best and most catholic of
philosophic thinkers. Indeed, it was more real
than Jesus. He, and not the dæmon dominions,
was the doubtful element. For us the whole
thing has vanished, like the baseless fabric of
a dream. We do not believe it. We think no
more of it, neither about Satan, nor his hosts.
But if the legend of spirits at war was a part
of the early Christian faith, what becomes of
Jesus? Is he going too, along with the rest
of the strange tales, to take his place among
the old imaginings? No; Jesus abides and
grows, first, because he is rooted in historic
fact, as actual and well attested a figure in
history as any one of us. Men knew him, saw
him, spoke with him. He was as definitely historical as Cæsar himself. Second, he abides

because, even today, he is more real than any of us, revealed in the depth, intensity, and fulness of his experience both of the dark facts of life and of the reality of God. Further, he abides because he is still unexhausted; because the race has not yet used to the full his experience of life and his intuitions of God. There is no example in history of a great personality putting a lesson to the world and passing away before the lesson is learned to the very end, and transcended. So far from transcending Jesus, we are still far, very far, behind him. The closing passages of the sermon were memorable, as much for their vital insight as for the quiet, compelling earnestness of the preacher; so much so that, looking toward the pulpit, we saw no man but Jesus only.

So far as I understand these modern times in which we live, religion is only possible to the modern man along the lines of Jesus Christ. For you and me there are no other religions. Of course, there are people who play at being Buddhists and Hindus; and we may wonder what the reflective Buddhist and the reflective Hindu think of them. All sorts of poses are adopted by men and women, but serious thinkers do not pose, and any man who comes to grips with history and philosophy knows that Buddha and Mohammed and the Hindu sages are not for us. It is Jesus or nobody, and we have not exhausted what he has to say. The plain fact is that God for Jesus, God in Jesus, is an unexplored treasure still; and for us, apart from Jesus, God is little better than an abstract noun; and, as I grow older, I find abstract nouns of less and less use. Let us put it this way. If we spoke straight out we should say that God could not do better than follow the example of Jesus. That means that Jesus fulfils our conception of God, but that is not enough. He is constantly enlarging our idea of God, revealing great tracts of God unsuspected by us. God interpretable in and through Jesus is unexhausted by you and me. That means that Jesus is going to stay.

I have not touched the fourth point yet, which is less theoretical than any of the others. There are about us hundreds of men and women who have found that in the terrible business of keeping level with life in the more terrible business of fighting one's character through to something like decency, Jesus is still a dependable factor. We are not dealing with propositions in the air; we are dealing with Someone to whom we can go and say, "Come and help me," and he does. If some of the psychologists will not quite let us say that, they must concede that we find help when we bring him in. In other words, where you touch Jesus you touch the real still. Is not that true? Do you not know men and women who have been remade by Jesus Christ? In your own lives, too, you know that help that Jesus has been and is. The fact that you can depend upon him, that you can utilise him, means that he stays.

My last point is this: If all this is so, do not we feel again the importance of keeping the gaze fixed upon him? That beautiful verse in Hebrews speaks of "Looking away and fixing the eyes upon Jesus"—keeping full in the forefront, not a theological figure, but the real, one, true, vivid Jesus; yesterday and today the same, and forever; tender, intelligent, sympathetic, wonderful, available; just the kind of Jesus to whom people went with every sort of trouble, lost children, the storm at sea, all sorts and kinds of things; the Jesus who could be interrupted by mothers with little children; and like it; the Jesus who took his friends away and lay under the trees with them when they were tired; the Jesus who knew their problems and helped them. Let us remember in all our thinking that Jesus in glory—and I do not know much about glory—is the same, and is to be interpreted by those stories of his life which we know so well in the gospels, and that he is not more inaccessible now than he was then, but better proved, better attested, better known, and more available for you and me. "Who shall separate us from the love of Christ?"

Of course the volume discussing *Jesus in the Experience of Men,* as we now have it, contains much more than the eight sermons delivered in Westminster Chapel. All the sermons were recast and extended, losing much in essay form, and the story of the Good Shepherd was omitted entirely—much to my regret.[1] Six other chapters were added, none more arresting than the one entitled "The Compromising Church," in which we hear a layman speaking very plainly about the narrowness and cowardice of the church. The complaint of educated people, he says, is that the church, for all its talk, is unsympathetic with progress

[1] In a later book, entitled *The Pilgrim,* made up of various articles and sketches, I am glad to see that Dr. Glover has included the story of the Good Shepherd, referred to above. Somehow, in spite of its richness of thought and insight, *Jesus in the Experience of Men* does not have the same satisfying appeal as *The Jesus of History* did. A young English minister states the matter briefly in a letter: "The simple, searching style of sentence is missing for the most part; there is a hesitancy of thought, a subconscious bewilderment, as though the subject was too great to handle—as indeed it is, since the whole world could hardly contain the books that could be written on such a theme. Dr. Glover, as historian, describes the world with the light of the Master's presence around him; but he fails when he turns to describe the light itself. The reader has the feeling that he is being led to a new focus of experience, but when he has finished the book he is still waiting for the promise which the writer holds out. Yet there are sentences that stick in the mind: 'The death of Jesus lit up the heart of God': 'The stars themselves move on the lines of Jesus': 'Prescribed thinking is proscribed thinking.' "

and with intellectual advance. It is mistrustful of art, and afraid of science and socialism; it clings to out-of-date scholarship and pre-Christian psychology, and presses philanthropy without economics and missions without anthropology. So far from representing Jesus to the world, it has made him odious to the intelligent mind. He does not mince matters in denouncing the alliance of English religion with special privilege, and its economic orthodoxy. Its weak spot has always been its uncertainty what to make of Jesus, and its unwillingness to obey him. "Its associations tainted with capitalism; its creed mere jargon —what is to help the church?" he asks. Still, he has faith in the church triumphant—when the church has dropped its reluctance to take Jesus seriously, when it believes he means what he says, and when it is willing to believe that Jesus and truth will prevail.

Such is the preaching of a great layman, who is also a great scholar, a historian of authority, and the Public Orator of the University of Cambridge. Even these excerpts from a single sermon show how real and vital his preaching is. There is hardly any man now living from whom preachers may learn more, except in his manner of delivery, and that is soon forgotten in the vividness of his insight and appeal. Few men unite as he does those three rarest of gifts, accurate knowledge, the ability to describe what he knows as if it were a new discovery, and to do so in words which anybody can understand. One of the greatest of living scholars, he is the least bookish of men, and the learned and the unlearned alike hear him gladly. His amazing knowledge never obscures the freshness of his vision. The Life of Jesus loses much of its power by sheer familiarity; we know it so well that we hardly know it at all. But when Dr. Glover writes of the Jesus of History, the old, old story is so real, so living, that we seem almost to be listening to it for the first time. Arnold says that Gray doubled his force by his style. The same is true of Dr. Glover, whose style is as lucid, as virile, as direct as his thought, and withal rich in rhythm and colour, with now a flash of crimson and now a gleam of gold. Above all, he bases himself on experience; in all his preaching the emphasis falls on fact that can be tested and relied on. No man can hear him without feeling that he is dealing with realities, and that he will not go an inch beyond what he sees to be verifiable and true.

There are those who say that the preaching of Dr. Glover, and his religious thinking in general, is too individualistic. It is a strange criticism to one who knows his writings, as, for example, his Angus lectures on *The Christian Tradition and its Verification,* in which his appeal, as always, is to the Christian experience of the ages, communal and cumulative, as against the errors of individual insight. Better still, because in briefer form, is the Swarthmore lecture on *The Nature and Purpose of a Christian Society:* a little gem, worth its weight in gold. When asked why, in a lecture delivered to a Yearly Meeting of the Society of Friends, he took such a turn, he said that he did it deliberately and of set purpose, in order to appeal to the experience of the historic church; whereas the Quaker differentia is, for the most part, an appeal against the historic church, "the apostasy," in fact, to quote George Fox. For, he added, "I believe that any real light that comes to man from God, directly or indirectly, will be confirmed by the light that

comes to others from him. It is for some such
reason that I appeal to the experience of the
historic church." As a study of the experience
of the church, its creative fellowship, the type
of character and quality of personality it has
produced, as well as the body of truth which
has been, and remains, its unique treasure, it
would be hard to name another little book
like it.

However, it is with Dr. Glover the preacher
—not the scholar, the historian, or the literary
critic—that we have now to do; doubly so because he is a layman, and ministers need to
know what kind of sermons a great layman
preaches. As a further example, and one showing not only the depth and simplicity of his
faith, but also his skill in direct appeal, in the
use of familiar language, and his habit of
avoiding the set phrases of theology, let us
take one of the noblest sermons of which I
have any knowledge, entitled "Why Jesus is
My Master." Five reasons are given for his
willingness to be called a "slave" of Jesus.
Being a man of modern education—critical,
hesitating, sceptical—he finds that intellectually
Jesus is the clearest and sincerest Teacher that

man has. It does not matter that he lived long
ago. It is not the date, but the depth that
counts, and Jesus went to the bottom of things
once for all. The lucidity of his moral vision
is only equalled by his faith in man. Indeed,
he is the only teacher who really offers any
hope for humanity, any way out of the pit of
personal and social sin. What is more to the
point, he not only has hope for man, but he has
the power to pick us up and set us on our feet
when we slip and fall into the mire. His magic
of personality, and his skill in making and leading men, compel his abject surrender and
devotion.

Who is the leader that you want to find?
What sort of a spirit? How does he handle
men? You know the difference between one
man and another; how one may steal a horse
and the other may not look over the hedge.
Why? Because it is he that takes the horse;
it is just him. That is not grammar perhaps,
but it is human experience. What is it about
him? somebody asks. I do not know, but it
is in him. Here is a story—a true one. It
comes from Italy, from one of the great periods
of Garibaldi. He had conquered Sicily for
Italy, he had conquered a large part of the
Neapolitan kingdom on the mainland, and was

held up on a river. A well-known Englishman
drifted into the camp, and while strolling about
came upon a soldier in rags. The terms in
which Garibaldi enlisted his men were these:
he paid them nothing, he gave them no clothes,
he gave them no food, and if they looted the
Italians he shot them. The Englishman got
to talking with the boy in rags about the situation. Yes, he was depressed. He said: "The
other day, as I was sitting here on the hill, I
was wondering how long I could stand it, or
whether I would go, desert. Things had got so
far, then he came by. I had never spoken to
him. But he saw me and came up to me, and
clapped me on the shoulder and said, 'Courage,
tomorrow we shall fight for our country!' Do
you think I could go after that?"

Now, what is that? We call it personal
magnetism. I do not know quite what that
means; it is just a long way of saying, "It's
him." That is the reason why Jesus enlists
people to stand with him. There is something
about him that, as you get to know him, makes
it impossible to have anything but enthusiasm
for him. The more you know of him the more
He is. The great regret of a Christian man
is that he has not served him enough; that he
has not more to give him. That is the experience of the Christian church. It is always
the Person: the highest thing we can guess of
God, his personality. And here is one who
comes into our midst, a person full of power

and charm. He takes our lives and makes good things out of them. He takes our temptations and beats them down under our feet. He forgives our sins; he restores us; goes with us, loves us and is ours. Do you wonder why men and women want to be called the slaves of Jesus Christ?

I want to put this to some of you: Can you face up to what he is? Can you see what he has done for men? What he has made of men, what he has enabled them to do, the way in which he has used them for the everlasting happiness and betterment of the race? Can you see that and say, "I do not think he has anything for me?" He has, and that is the gospel; that he who enlisted others, charmed them, kept them, used them, is going to enlist you, and he is going to do with you more than you dream. How old are you? Eighteen? Forty? Fifty? There is no telling what Jesus Christ can do with a man or woman once they have surrendered. What I urge is that you surrender to him. That is all.

X: S. Parkes Cadman

In writing about Dr. Cadman, even if one shares his breadth of sympathy, one craves something of his rare gift of insight and characterisation; the more because he is so baffling to all analysis. He admires widely, and with catholic appreciation; he can praise both Lacordaire and Gipsy Smith, and is as much at home with Newman as with Wesley. At once generous and discerning, dynamic and gentle, he is so many-sided, so fertile, so amazing in his activities, and withal so human and lovable, that he puzzles any artist because he is so unlike any model. The spaciousness and majesty of his thought, the swiftness and felicity of his delivery, the enchantment of his personality, leave one with a sense of dismay. Some years ago an English friend, having heard Dr. Cadman at Whitefield's in the morning and Dr. Gunsaulus at the City Temple in the evening, confided to me his impressions:

Two of your prophets held central citadels in "ye olde London town" today, much to our edification. They differ as much from each other in type as do the men whose pulpits they occupied, Horne and Campbell; but both are princes of the invisible. Cadman is not an impressive figure in the pulpit—until he begins to speak. Then the whole man lights up. His voice has some unusual tone qualities and rare carrying power. Sturdy, broad of shoulder, with close-cropped brown hair touched with grey, he is as decisive in movement as he is direct in speech. He speaks, through his whole personality, of energy and intellect. His closely knit argument, his still more closely knit sentences, finely phrased but delivered with passionate rapidity, overwhelm by the power of reason at white heat. An excerpt is like an amputation. A note directly opposite, but not opposed, is struck by Gunsaulus, who is an impressionist artist in words, relying more on illustration and colour. The sermon of Cadman was that of an architect producing a splendid effect as a whole by infinite attention to detail. Gunsaulus is a man of large, strong gesture, of lyrical speech, in which a haunting voice and poetic thought blend to win by beauty rather than compel by power. He is dramatic rather than argumentative. Something of the crooning magnetism of Gipsy Smith is tempered in him by a large and rich culture. Cadman revealed throughout his extraordinary power of literary phrasing, and if the impression he makes is more intellectual than spiritual, it is both virile and challenging. America is happy in having two men of such rare gifts, one on the eastern seaboard and the other in the Middle West.

Unfortunately, Dr. Cadman has published no volume of sermons, so far as I am aware;[1] and one must depend upon newspaper reports—especially those in the *Brooklyn Eagle,* which is in fact a great pulpit with one Amen Corner in New England and the other in Florida, with the Rocky Mountains for a gallery. For a long time, though I had heard Dr. Cadman lecture, I knew him as a preacher only in his reported sermons, and that is hardly to know him at all, since there is so much in the personality of the man—Rooseveltian in its

[1] One does not forget his brilliant volume of lectures, *Charles Darwin and other English Thinkers;* as valuable for its portrayal of the background and setting of the men studied, as for its analysis of their thought. Some of us think *The Three Religious Leaders of Oxford* the best bit of work Dr. Cadman has done, showing his powers put forth at full stretch on themes congenial to his mind and heart. No one may ever hope to find a more satisfying study of Wesley, the wonder of whose life remains as baffling as it is fascinating—as if Benjamin Franklin had become the greatest evangelist since St. Paul. Dr. Denney, in his *Letters,* renews our amazement, but does not solve the riddle of it. If Dr. Cadman leaves the mystery of Newman unsolved, it is because no one can unravel it until the secrets of all hearts are known.

energy, enthusiasm, and winsomeness—that
does not find its way into print. So it was
nothing short of a revelation when I went for
the first time to Central Church—the "Tin
Church," as it is called in Brooklyn—taking
with me a discerning friend who boasts his
ability as a sermon-taster, and not without
good reason, for he listened to Beecher for
fifteen years.

The Church was full, though not crowded;
the audience for the most part middle-aged
people, and the men were in the majority—
hard-headed business and professional men
apparently. The service was planned and conducted by a man who is not simply a preacher,
but a minister, and in the highest and best sense
a sacramentarian; sane enough to achieve richness of worship without too much ritual—just
as he is wise enough to be liberal yet evangelical
in faith. There was about the man, as Carlyle
would say, somewhat of the Eternal. When
he began the sermon one felt that he regarded
the sermon as also a sacrament, not a rostrum
for a reputation but an opportunity to lead
men to God; and that he loves men too well
to lead them anywhere else. There he stood,

a stockily-built figure, the very embodiment of mental efficiency and spiritual sanity, reminding me of a passage in a book of science describing the quality called vigour, which is evidently something more than strength, something more than health; a capacity for living intensely, yet without any loss of balance, a power of expending energy lavishly yet without ceasing to have plenty in reserve, an ability to resist strain and to defy fatigue. It implies being ever ready for great exertions and yet having staying power.

The sermon was entitled "Treasures in Christ"—Col. 2:3—and it was no haphazard affair, but a real work of homiletic art, orderly in arrangement, exquisite in language, apt in illustration; but its art was forgotten in the effortless ease—nay, more, the rejoicing urgency—with which it was delivered. It had a skeleton and was athletic enough to stand alone, but so much alive that its bones did not stick out in Firstly, Secondly, and so forth. It was a characteristic Cadman sermon, as much for its vitality as for its distinction of manner; moving in a large orbit, bright with insight and epigram, and reminding one of

David Swing in the great names with which it conjured. Its daring and far-ranging generalisations seemed to open new vistas of divine surprise, until we saw Christianity as the centre and synthesis of truth; a faith simple, catholic, profound, satisfying the thinker and alone equal to the problem of redemption in its tragic and gigantic modern setting. After the first ten minutes my friend the sermon-taster said it was glorified glibness; at the end he thought it nothing less than miraculous. And no wonder; for it was a portrayal of the uniqueness, comprehensiveness, and supremacy of the living Christ, as certain of its sentences, which my friend can still quote, make plain:

We reflect upon the blind gropings and blurred apprehension of venerable faiths. Their literature is translated and we read it with curious and pathetic interest. The scurvy gods of the pantheons, vindictive and weak, are condemned and repudiated by us. Men may be agnostic, they may become atheists, but never again can men apprentice themselves to these primitive forms. In the teaching of Jesus these erstwhile faiths find explanation. They are part of the cosmic process in religion: tragic, but significant, overtures ere the Lord of men appears to bring them to God. He gives to nature heart and purpose. He shows that the very ground beneath our feet is sympathetic, that no star shines or pales away without his consent. This earthly scene becomes intelligible in him, and pain and sorrow and death cannot be understood apart from his word concerning them.

No wonder that Christian theology is hastening, under pressure, to restore central authority to the doctrine of the incarnation. Christ himself, no book, no creed, no ecclesiastical form, has seized the life of this age, so vast, so complex and so baffling, and now, as never, history gives him testimony and the ages chant: "Thou hast the words of eternal life." If you ask why this changeless power over society exists in Jesus, the only reply is, because He ever lives as a present authority. Other masters are an echo; He is a voice. They died and left their systems to the blemish of time; He controls the event by being with its happening. Hence the adaptations of the religion He founded among different races. Christianity began in Rome, hidden in the catacombs, and upward it came to rear into Italy's pure and brilliant skies its monuments of faith.

Much of the treasure is hidden, but since the treasures are hidden in Christ, they are as safe as He is and as abiding as His eternity. The mighty strands of Brooklyn Bridge are gathered into one great heart of masonry at either end, and there buried out of sight, and we cross

the stream in safety. So the complex web of
life, its apparent antinomies, its grief, its pain,
its ministries, its explanations, are gathered up
into the mighty heart of Jesus, and whatever
wonder awaits man, however fecund his dis-
coveries and phenomenal his advances, he will
continue to cross the gulfs of time in safety,
since life, knowledge and wisdom are hidden
with Christ in God, to whom be glory forever
and ever.

Next evening we met to read and discuss the
sermon, but, alas, the report of it in the *Eagle*
was only an elaborate synopsis, hardly more
than a thin shadow of what we had heard.
Moreover it read less like a sermon than a
lecture, or an article in a Review; so much does
the work of Dr. Cadman lose when his personality is withdrawn. Something was lost.
Glamour was not the word to describe it, because it suggests something unreal, and the
spell which he cast over us was not only real,
but exalting and revealing. However, we
agreed—reading a number of his sermons in
the glow of that radiance—that he was one
of the best natural orators we had ever heard,
for his grace, ease, fluency, fertility, and resource, having a copious vocabulary, rich in

content and quality—albeit lacking at times in the reticences and reserves which true style requires. Also, his studentship, at once prodigious and omniverous, filled us with astonishment, and what he had read was assimilated and minted in his own mind. Indeed, he is one of the few popular preachers who really cares for learning, and his knowledge is encyclopediacal in its accuracy and range. As a maker of sermons he is unique, alike in his style and his skill, but hardly the equal of his neighbour, Dr. Hillis, as a master of popular homiletics. Strong, vivid, full-blooded—the Rubens of the pulpit, as Jowett is its Meissonier—he is a great preacher for the greatness of his themes, no less than for the virility of his thought and faith; and because he always leaves us thinking and wondering, not about himself—his brilliant mind, his incisive reasoning, his lambent eloquence—but about the great things of life; about God and man, about following Christ, about the crown of sanctity and the building of that city which hath foundations.

Of books about preaching by great preachers we have had many, and the value of each, aside from the fresh wisdom of experience which it

teaches, lies in the unconscious self-revelation
of its author. It is always interesting to see
how a master workman does his work, though
not much that is new has been said about the
technique of preaching since Phelps and
Broadus; and little has been added to its history
and philosophy since Dykes, Dargan, and Beh-
rends. Brilliant, stimulating, wise in practical
counsel, fruitful alike in generalisation and
in characterisation, the lectures of Dr. Cadman, *Ambassadors of God,* are disappointing
in their personal communicativeness, as compared, for example, with the lectures of
Beecher, Jefferson, or Quayle. However, it
was not his purpose to add a new vade-mecum
to an already long catalogue; but, rather, to
give a swift survey of the history, philosophy
and practice of preaching, the better to show
its function in these new and strange times.
No man among us is better fitted, both by
knowledge and sure-footed wisdom, to guide
his brethren amid the bewildering eddies, cross-
currents, and whirlpools of modern life and
thought; and therein lies the chief value of the
book. He is a Greatheart threading the
tangled maze of the modern mind, astray in

its own confusion, and telling us that there is nothing to dishearten the preacher of Christ in the agitations and misapprehensions of this ambiguous age. Unfortunately, the style of the lectures, "loaded with polysyllabic Latinity," is often a disadvantage, and at times as ponderous as procession of elephants. This is due, in large part, to the fact that for Dr. Cadman—as for Beecher—writing is a drudgery, and so much that is most commanding and winsome in the man breaks through words and escapes. Had the lectures been reported they would have been ten times better—aglow with flashes of lightning and every kind of felicity and surprise, which only an audience can evoke from the preacher. Despite this limitation, no better book about the great art, which is also an incarnation, has come to us in many a day. An exalted conception of the office of preaching, a romantic sense of its history, rich experience, wide reading, and a vision of the need and challenge of a world troubled, enthralled, groping, unite to give us an overwhelming sense of the divine origin, worth, and permanent function of the gospel ministry. Much needed, too, especially in

America, is the emphasis upon preaching as itself sacramental, and the insistence that the sermon is not a thing apart, but a passage in the context of the worship which it seeks to inspire, direct, and interpret.

Some things Dr. Cadman ought to explain to his brethren, and one is the secret by which he seems to have all that he has ever heard, read or thought instantly at command, as if he had it pigeonholed in his mind within reach. It is almost uncanny. There is a sentence in the *Life of John Sterling,* by Carlyle, which describes it exactly: "So ready lay his store of knowledge round him, so perfect was his ready utterance of the same—in coruscating wit, in jocund drollery, in compact articulated clearness or high poignant emphasis, as the case required—he was a match for any man in argument before a crowd." Hence a ministry of information, no less than of inspiration, in which Dr. Cadman is surpassed by no living man. He reads everything and forgets nothing; and his ability to summon all his resources at will—added to his amazing industry in study, his painstaking preparation, and his incredible gift of speech—make him one of the great public teachers of his time. Nothing human is alien to Dr. Cadman, and his interpretative insight and picturesque eloquence mark him as without doubt the most brilliant and effective popular lecturer since Beecher— a Christian publicist, a former of intelligent national opinion, an incomparable champion of fraternal righteousness and practical idealism, whose personality is an invaluable asset to the republic.

In Brooklyn, Dr. Cadman is not simply a personality; he is an institution. Not alone as orator, but as pastor, organiser, citizen, and friend, he is a leader whose authority is only equalled by his sanity, and his church is a community force. Keeping his pose in a difficult time, weighing the issues carefully, thrilling in appeal, terrific in denunciation, during the great war he was a tower of strength, not only in his own city, but all over the land. If a vexed question agitates the public mind, or some united public effort is needed in behalf of the public good, it is Dr. Cadman who crystallises the sentiment and best judgment of the community. His conferences for men at the Bedford Branch of the Young Men's

Christian Association have been for years both a local and a national forum, and a feature of Greater New York. Week after week he holds a vast audience of men—perhaps the largest in the country—discussing an astonishing range of subjects, and in addition answering questions dealing with every conceivable topic, from the character of Socrates to the Passion Play at Hoboken. There he is in his glory, and his replies, if sometimes oracular, are compounded of accurate knowledge, sanctified common sense, and sparkling wit, equally a joy to the student and a terror to the crank. For example:

Q—Do you believe in the Darwinian theory of evolution, and do you think it explains anything?

A—According to that theory, man is not only descended from the ape, but he has within him a whole menagerie, and sometimes the ape is uppermost, and sometimes the ass. I am inclined to believe in it; it explains a lot.

Q—Who was the greatest man, Cæsar, Alexander, Cromwell, or Isaac Newton?

A—If true greatness consists in the right use of a powerful understanding, Sir Isaac Newton leads the list. It is to such men as Newton—men who enlighten their fellow men

—not to men who enslave them by violence, that we owe reverence.

Q—What was the ideal of the Pilgrim Fathers, and why do you attribute supremacy to them in the making of America?

A—A theocracy consisting of a solemn allegiance to the covenant of the gospel and a determination to walk by its rule, whatever the cost. The Pilgrim was supreme because his ideals were the loftiest and he made the largest sacrifices in their behalf. It was reserved for a band of obscure and despised sectaries to lay down in all essentials the principles of representative democracy. They set sail from the old world, but they carried a new world in their hearts.

Q—What is the matter with the church? Where are the great preachers, such as we used to have?

A—Internally, sectarian strife; externally, the prevalent indifference and the superficial character of much of the national mind. Preaching has killed the Christian church. We go to church to hear the star in the pulpit. We have become sermon tasters instead of Christian workers. You hear a fat old grocer boast that he has sat under the pulpit of Rev. Blowhard for twenty years, and all the time you know that he has been skinning the public. We are a sorry lot and make a poor fist at religion.

Q—Has Christianity failed? After two

thousand years of its influence why are we in
such a mess?

A—No; Christianity has not failed; as Chesterton said, it has been found difficult and laid
aside. I should like to see a demonstration of
its efficiency in every sort of man, using the
leading churches for the occasion. Get together the regenerated Pharisees, the converted
nobodies, the saved who were once lost and far
away from God. Let the preacher for once
retire. What eloquence could equal the story
of such transformed lives! The outcome would
be that many of us would perceive that the
same power that brought St. Paul to the feet
of Jesus, that sent Henry Martyn to India and
Father Damien to the lepers, that touched the
tongues of St. Bernard and of Beecher, is an
everlasting power and has signs and wonders
attending it.

So wholesome, so intelligently loyal, so nobly
prophetic is the Americanism of Dr. Cadman,
that one has difficulty in remembering his British origin. None the less, because he married
a wife he does not hate his old mother, and no
small part of his remarkable ministry is the
service he has rendered in behalf of the friendship of English-speaking peoples. Here, too,
he has been an Ambassador of God, embodying,
as he does, the common spirit and ideal of

kindred lands. No doubt William James would classify Dr. Cadman among the "tough-minded," rather than among the mystics; but he would rejoice in his brilliant intellect, his abounding vitality, his buoyant good cheer, and his infinite brotherliness, which knows no bounds of creed, or sect, or party—all the rich human qualities which make him so radiant and so fascinating. No man is more beloved by his brethren, as much for his goodness of heart as for his gifts of mind, all of whom have an honourable Christian pride in a ministry as fruitful in personal blessing as it is nation wide in its influence.

XI: Reginald J. Campbell

No two men were ever more unlike in physical aspect, intellectual quality and spiritual appeal, than the first two ministers of the City Temple. The first was a sturdy, stockily built giant, the second slight, frail, almost ethereal; one the son of a stone-mason, the other a child of the manse; an old man with a black mane followed by a young man with a white mane. If one had a rugged, massive, dynamic intellect, the other had a mystical mind of iridescent brilliance. One personality was pervasive, opulent, diffusive, the other magnetic, absorbent, winsome. The eloquence of the older man had always a suggestion of the stage, not that it was insincere, but because the dramatic instinct was ineradicable; the oratory of the younger man was unaffected in its simplicity, with no effort after effect, and no flowers of rhetoric. The contrast might go on indefinitely, they were so utterly different; yet each in his own distinction and power was a man of mark, and each had a word of God for his age.

Mark Rutherford thought that George Mac-Donald was the most fascinating preacher that ever entered a pulpit: but if he had seen the young man who came up from Brighton, at the dying wish of Joseph Parker, to the City Temple in 1902, he might have altered his verdict. With a head grey in youth, eyes eloquent with a nameless hunger, and a face thin and pallid as that of some ascetic of the desert, his advent in the pulpit was an event—one had almost said, an apparition. Seldom, if ever, has there been a figure more arresting, a presence more captivating, or an appeal more winning than R. J. Campbell made in those early days of his incandescence. Preaching, said Dr. Parker, will endure as long as the race, but it must be *preaching;* and the *Sermons Addressed to Individuals* were preaching of the most real kind, at once searching and revealing. The vestry of the City Temple is a confessional, as I well know, and each of the sermons dealt with some personal problem confided to the preacher, uniting a clairvoyant insight with a sympathy almost substitutionary. Direct, con-

crete, lambent, they were unique in their evoca-
tion of the religious atmosphere, and in that
"naturalization of the Unseen" which it is the
glory of the pulpit to achieve.   If in their
printed form the sermons lost something, it was
because no art could detain the incommunicable grace of a personality as challenging as it
was charming.   From a letter dated 1904, written by a friend long vanished, I take these
words giving an impression of the "Little Grey
Angel," as the preacher was described:

A more beautiful countenance than his I
have never beheld among living men.   There
are pictures of the saints that possess the same
haunting and ethereal loveliness.   It is a beauty
that affects some men as being almost uncanny;
the features are so delicate that they would be
effeminate save for the glowing, searching eyes
and the firm, long lines of the chin.   The hair
is prematurely grey, but luxuriant.   Garbed in
his long black cassock, the preacher looked like
a Dante that had known no sorrow.   Asceticism
was there, but no hardness; spirituality without
aloofness.   As he stood in silence when he rose
to preach, searching out the people with his
eyes, he looked like a friendly angel.   His delivery was not good, being muffled and feeble,
sometimes dropping almost to a murmur.   He
seemed to use manuscript, but I got the impres-

sion that only notes and headings were written down. Frequently he made use of devotional poetry, summing up an argument or a plea with a stanza. He spoke intimately to the people and never waxed either oratorical or spectacular. The most extreme gesture that he made was a long, upward and outward movement of the arm, as though he intended to drop a thought among the rear pews. It was a curious and, as you may observe, not an easy gesture to describe, but it had a striking effect and brought the beholder up with a start. My impression all through was of a profound but quietly expressed solicitude that man should not only be happier for being good, but be better for being happier. The secret of his power is elusive. The explanation for such a lack of explanation would naturally be—magnetism or genius. The magnetism, certainly, is undeniable. As to the latter, it is doubtful whether his warmest friends would claim for him the title of genius. Ability, grace, charm, skill— yes; but genius—no.

Unfortunately, it was never my joy to hear Campbell in the City Temple in those days, and one had to see and hear him in that setting in order to know him at his best. Outside the Temple he seemed bereft of half his power, which explains the disappointment of those who heard him elsewhere, and especially in America.

Knowing something of the amazing audience
which assembles in the City Temple—amazing
alike in its composition and in its spiritual con-
trasts—I know how it tugs at the heart of the
preacher. The curious tourists who "do" the
Temple count for as little as the jaded sermon-
tasters seeking a new thrill. The standing
congregation is a mixed multitude in itself, too
bewilderingly varied to be described, with
which is joined a crowd of lonely, baffled folk,
drawn or driven by an inappeasable need of the
soul, and no preacher can ever forget their
eager, expectant, storm-vexed faces. Men
fighting for faith, men who have lost the fight,
spiritual derelicts tossed between cynicism and
despair—weary, unexcited, tormented—defeated men whose past is ever before them, and
women to whom hell is the only reality—these
sit side by each at every service. The appeal to
the penetrative and compassionate understanding of the preacher is like "deep calling unto
deep," and if he has the shepherd soul it is
irresistible. To such an audience—its mind a
chaos of unrelated ideas, its soul dumb with a
wordless yearning, terrible in the loneliness of
a great city—Campbell came like an old mystic

who had wandered out of the Middle Ages. Without being æsthetically fine or intellectually satisfying, his presence was electrifying, his personality haunting, his utterance thrilling—

Clothed about with flame and with tears, and
    singing
Songs that break the heart of the earth with
    pity.

Such was the minister of the City Temple when the New Theology sensation began: a matter with which I have not to do, except to say that, since it was neither new nor a theology, it did not enlist my interest. Indeed, we in America were amazed at the furor it made, finding in it little, if anything, that had not long been familiar to us either in the old liberalism or the new orthodoxy; nothing, that is, unless it was a misplaced emphasis or a sense of proportion all awry. It seemed to us only another proof of the saying of Disraeli that the English are the most enthusiastic and least excitable people on earth, and that the two inspirations of their enthusiasm are politics and religion. Nor did we on this side realise that the movement had been taken up by the

Northcliffe papers, especially by the *Daily Mail,*
which exploited an ethereal personality in a
manner unprecedented—taking bits of his sermons out of their context and flashing them in
large type, much to the regret of the preacher
and his friends. The book entitled *The New
Theology,* and described in its preface as "a
concise statement of the outlines of the teaching given from the City Temple pulpit," while
containing many vagrant insights of rare
beauty, was so ill-considered and hastily written as almost to justify the cartoon in *Punch,*
showing the author pacing up and down his
study, dictating a new theology in an evening.

There is no wish on my part to belittle the
author of *The New Theology;* far from it.
He was a preacher of rare and exquisite art,
commanding many resources, and there was
always a suggestion of a supernatural background to his ministry. His knowledge of the
human heart—especially in its bafflements, its
struggle with temptation, its pain at the hardness of life, its wistful loneliness—was almost
uncanny; and his divination of what people
were thinking and feeling, of their inarticulate
yearnings, made him an answerer of the un-

asked questions of many minds. His preaching during the New Theology days was in many ways extraordinary, albeit marred at times by an aggressive self-consciousness. Often a sermon began with a too elaborate, if not laboured, exegesis of the text in the light of the higher criticism—"I believed the Germans too readily," he afterwards said—but it nearly always found focus in a glow-point of real insight. His prayers, too, were singularly searching, healing, exalting. Indeed, many were drawn to him, not because he had invented a new theology, but because, with real insight and at the psychological moment, he uttered truths deeply felt, or dimly seen, in the terms of his time, and related Christianity to everyday life and the issues of his age. His spiritual fervour, his moral earnestness, his passion for social justice found response in many who knew little, and cared less, about any kind of theology, new or old.

Nor do I mean to imply that the New Theology movement, at one time so much discussed, did no good except to make a stir in the dry leaves. It did good both directly and indirectly. It awakened interest in religion; it emphasised

the social meaning of Christianity; it enabled
many ministers to speak their minds more
freely and frankly; and a freer, fresher air was
felt to be blowing through all the churches.
Though the movement itself has had its day
and ceased to be, thousands of people were
made aware of a new sense of reality and a new
impulse to service.   The leader of the New
Theology reached the zenith of his influence
and power in 1909, and the following year was
smitten with a serious illness which seemed to
affect not only his body but his whole personality.   Three sermons a week, besides innumer-
able outside demands, had overtaxed his
strength.   The minister of the City Temple, as
I learned to my sorrow, is regarded as public
property in London, and it is a wonder to me
that so frail a man as Campbell stood the strain
as long as he did.   A second visit to America
in 1911 did not improve his health, but it
marked the turning point of his career.   A
subtle change crept into his pulpit utterances,
and the congregations at the City Temple,
while still relatively large, began to decline.
At the Thursday noon service the attendance
became smaller than it has been for thirty

years. Another illness in July, 1914, left the
preacher unspeakably frail, and in the autumn
he resigned and entered the Church of England.

Dr. Parker had left a large and influential
following at the City Temple, but the attrition
of years, the changes in London, and, more
than all, the agitations of the succeeding ministry, scattered it. Not a few left when the
New Theology discussion began, and many
more when the minister adventured into socialism. Others took their places, to be sure, in-
cluding a multitude of young people who filled
the Temple with ardour and enthusiasm. But
when their leader recanted his teaching they, in
turn, were first dazed, and then disillusioned,
like sheep led into a wilderness and deserted
by the shepherd—surely not the least part of
the tragedy of a notable career. As a result
little was left at the City Temple: as one of its
officers said to me when I arrived: "It is not
only flat, it is a hole in the ground." When I
took up my labours at the Temple my predeces-
sor was a priest of St. Philip's Cathedral, in
Birmingham, and had just published his apologia, entitled *A Spiritual Pilgrimage*. It

was more than an apology; it was a recantation. Perhaps an Intellectual Pilgrimage had been a better title; but the tone of the book was irenic, with very few barbed sentences, yet one felt all through a deep undercurrent of disappointment. He spoke rather sadly of "my most latitudinarian days," meaning his great days at the City Temple, over which he wished to "draw a veil." Indeed, he was not aware of owing anything in his religious life to Nonconformist influences; what he had received from that source was rather "a truer view of history and of the sterner realities of modern life."

He was explicit in his remarks about his *"re-ordination,"* a word not chosen at haphazard, when he said that he believed himself to be "no more, and no less, truly a minister of Jesus Christ after I had been ordained in the Church of England than I was before"; and he regarded that act as no judgment upon his ministry one way or the other. "The fact is that distinctive nonconformist—or shall I say evangelical?—theology failed me," he said. Apparently the New Theology had failed him, too. He felt, as he frankly admitted, that "in the corporate unity of the catholic church and in that alone was full satisfaction to be found for my religious need." Yet he makes the curious remark that had his health stood the strain, he did not see how he could legitimately, "in all reason and conscience," have left the City Temple. Indeed, he more than once said to me that if he could have had an assistant, as I had at the City Temple, he would not have left. It was all very strange, and the apologia did not explain it.

Nor is it my business to inquire into it further.[1] Later, when Mr. Campbell came to London as Vicar of Christ Church, Westminster, I found him the same lovable and brotherly man whom I had met and heard in America, albeit somewhat pensive and aloof— as one who had "journeyed a long way and passed many graves along the road." At the invitation of a mutual friend, I attended his

---

[1] It was not so much the fact of his entering another communion that hurt the people of the City Temple—though to some of his friends it was like a personal bereavement—but the way in which it was done. He could have had anything he asked—never was a man more beloved—but the church was not taken into confidence. His arrangements for entering the Established Church were made before his friends knew anything about it. He had a right to burn all bridges behind him, but so loyal a people deserved a better fate.

Induction as Vicar, and I shall not soon forget
my feelings when I saw him stand at the altar,
holding a Bible aloft in his hand, and accept
the Thirty-nine Articles of faith—remembering what he had often said of the intellect
capable of such a feat. Many great and saintly
men accept that ancient formula, but for Mr.
Campbell to do so required a reversal of mind
which baffled his friends and puzzled his foes.
In all this he was utterly sincere—being a man
who lives in phases—but I wondered what had
happened in his heart, and how such a thing
could be. Temperament, no doubt, explains
much. The very qualities which made him so
stimulating a preacher unfitted him as a guide
for theological wayfarers, the more so when,
unfixed from his orbit, he became a wandering
star. For he was ever a lonely, pilgrim soul,
"a trail of fire burning at white heat," restless,
impulsive, erratic.[2] Such a mind has no place
in English Nonconformity, in which there is
so much that is not only definite, but hard, unyielding, and, if one may say so, ungracious.
By temperament, no less than by training, R. J.
Campbell belongs in the Church of England,

[2] *Prophets, Priests, and Kings,* by A. G. Gardiner.

and no one will begrudge him the peace he has found in its wide fellowship, its sweet and tempered ways, and its veneration for those forms and symbols which enshrine the wisdom and faith of the past.

Often, during his ministry at the City Temple, Mr. Campbell—Dr. Campbell, as he is now, by the grace of Oxford University—was urged to write a Life of Christ; no doubt because he made Christ a living reality to so many seeking and hitherto baffled souls. At last, after many delays due to the Great War, he has fulfilled that request; but it is not the great Life of Jesus for which we have been waiting, written in full light of the ancient faith and the new knowledge—for that the author has neither the scholarship nor the literary gift. In many respects his Life of Jesus is different from what it would have been had he written it while minister of the City Temple. His attitude and point of view have changed. The homiletic instinct prevails, and he promises to follow this volume with a homiletical commentary on the Gospels. Every man unconsciously portrays that in Christ most akin to himself; and in this volume Mr. Campbell is at his best when inter-

preting "the wonderful winsomeness" of the
Master, as Papini, who fell in love with Jesus
while reading the Gospels to the peasants, sees
him as "terribly and fearfully alone." The
book is rich in insight and beauty, making us
feel the majesty of the Master, and still more
the nameless and haunting charm which clings
to every word and gesture of those swift and
gentle years.

XII: William A. Quayle

Those who have read *Old Delabole,* by
Eden Phillpotts, will not soon forget the little
Cornish village—so near to the "sounding
shores of Boss and Bude"—where men win
with patient toil, and not without peril, the
famous dark grey slate that is the delight of
every good builder. But even to the dwellers
of that "City of Slate," the religious activities
of the village, divided between "Wesleyans"
and "Uniteds," take rank with the affairs of
the great quarry in interest and importance.
It is worth while to know Granfer Nute, the
village philosopher, who comes aptly to the
rescue of every perplexing situation with his
shrewd humour and his quaint estimates of men
and things. Foregathered one day with his
special crony, they discuss the aims and actions
of certain young people, as old folk are wont to
do:

"Pity your grandson hedn't more like his

brother Pooley, and not so fond of dolly-mopping with the girls," said the friend of the philosopher.

"Pooley has the Methodist mind," Granfer replied. "Ned hedn't. He's feeling out for the joy of life, while Pooley wants the joy of truth."

Not all may be willing to agree that there is a Methodist mind, as a thing distinct and set apart, on the ground that others have an equal right to Granfer's highly honourable phrase. However that may be, there is a Methodist genius, unique, particular, precious—joining mind and heart, uniting the joy of truth with the joy of life—and there has never been a more perfect incarnation of it than Bishop Quayle; in whom humour, pathos, literature, life, faith, philosophy and poetry are made incandescent by a spiritual genius who is also an unveneered human being. What he may be as an executive I know not—though it is reported that a great layman once thanked God "for one Bishop Quayle, and no more"—but as a preacher there is not another like him in Methodism, or anywhere else. In a church so rich in great preachers—the church of Simpson and

Fowler, of Price Hughes and W. L. Watkinson—no one may be supreme; but Bishop Quayle is one of the princes of that realm, a peer in a shining company of those whose hearts God has touched with light and power and loveliness. No wonder he confirms some of us in the conviction, long held as an article of faith, that when God made the Methodist Church he did not do anything else that whole day; and behold it was good!

Many times I have heard Bishop Quayle preach, before he was elevated to the episcopate and after, but one day stands out in my memory as showing the many-sidedness of the man. It was at a conference over which he presided in Iowa, and I can still see him as he stood transfigured by the autumn sunlight falling through a lovely window—tall, stockily built, stooped, his massive head crowned with reddish hair tinged with grey, his great blue eyes the homes of laughter and of tears, his face as mutable as the sea. As I entered the church, I heard first ripples and then roars of laughter, for no great preacher of our time makes so liberal a use of wit and humour in his work; bright wit in which there is no sting;

sweet humour without any acid. The bishop
was receiving a group of young men into the
ministry, to an accompaniment of a running
commentary on the requirements and duties of
a minister as laid down in the Discipline. Nothing was omitted, not even "the expectoratious
subject of tobacco," and neither before nor
since have I heard so much common sense
taught in the guise of nonsense. Among other
things he advised each minister to have a patch
of ground—large or small—all his own, where
he could take refuge from obstinate bishops
and obstreperous elders, and assert his rights.
We laughed until we cried as he described the
foibles of the minister, and the difficulties and
trivialities of his work; then we cried in earnest
as he spoke of the meaning of the ministry, its
dignity, its pathos, and its sacred service amid
the lights and shadows of life.

After the singing of a hymn, the bishop read
the account of the raising of Dorcas and
preached a sermon, which might have had for
its title the Wordsworth phrase, "The Deep
Power of Joy"—always a keynote in his preaching, and one too seldom heard in our anxious
modern days. It was a charge to the church

204 Some Living Masters of the Pulpit

in behalf of the young men whom he had welcomed into the ministry; a study of the atmosphere which the gospel of Christ should create —a happy, healing, redeeming atmosphere in which evil will be overcome as seeds of good grow into golden harvest. Since Christianity is a gospel of joy—no vague, mystical ecstasy, but a real, human-hearted joy—its messengers should be bringers of joy, changing the human climate from winter to summer. The sermon was an illustration of its subject. Serious but in nowise solemn, it created the very atmosphere it described—"almost a picnic spirit," as one listener called it—reminding me of the saying of Hermas, that the Holy Spirit is a hilarious spirit. For an hour the preacher made us glad about God—glad about life and the world —showing us that there is healing for all the hates and hurts of life, if we use the gospel with strategy and skill. As a feat of homiletics it was a work of art, albeit, like a vine-covered church, its solid structure was hidden by every kind of beauty both of imagery and of phrase. It was not rhetoric but poetry; and the manner of its delivery had all the freedom, directness and charm of a stump speech.

As if all that were not enough for one day, in the evening the bishop gave a lecture on *The Tale of Two Cities,* the like of which I have never heard from anyone else. It would have delighted Dickens, both for its vivid portraiture and its dramatic power, being a series of sketches of the characters in the story seen against the stupendous background of the Revolution. In speaking of Sidney Carton and his fight with the demon of drink, he let fall a page from his own life, telling how when only a lad of ten he lay drunk on the floor of a saloon. His mother was dead, his father was a miner at his work, and the rough men thought it a great joke to make the boy drunk. It made the heart shudder, and in his dealing with Carton one felt that he was aware of his own escape from a tragic fate. There was no need to point the moral, save in one swift sentence which flashed like a silver arrow as it hit the mark. Surely no one ever forgot that day of wonder, so fruitful in inspiration for the heart and in "pollen for the mind," to use one of its happy phrases. It was like an apocalypse in which the preacher stood revealed, equally in his homely counsel to his young brethren and in his high command of great assemblies; his tender humanity, his witchery of personality, his knowledge of life from bottom to top, his magic of speech, his love of the out-of-doors—a mind as full of colour as a painter's shop, a heart lyrically confident of God and joyously loyal to the Master.

A child of the Isle of Man, brought up in the large and liberal air of the Middle West of America, the life of Bishop Quayle, as one day it will be told, shows us the growth of a great preacher and the process of his making. How interesting it is to compare the earliest volume of his sermons, *Eternity in the Heart,* a fruit of his Kansas City ministry—happily left as they came from the heart and lips of the preacher on his feet—with his latest volume, entitled *The Dynamite of God,* and note the deeper insight and the greater wealth of beauty and suggestiveness. In the first volume there is hardly a literary allusion; in the second, there are almost too many. If only we had a volume between them, a trophy of his pastorate at St. James Church, Chicago, we might the better study the stages of the rapid unfolding of his vision and power; how he took all life and all literature as his province, levying tribute in the name of his Master. Yet it would be hard to name anything more brilliant than his fraternal address to the British Wesleyan Conference in 1902, though what I best remember about it is his unforgettable tribute to his father. Every man has his own idiom, which is the accent of his heart, the native gesture of his mind; but of late years Bishop Quayle has fallen into certain mannerisms of literary style which mar his work, giving at times almost an impression of artificiality—a thing utterly alien to his nature. In these despites, not since Joseph Parker went away have we had a preacher so epigrammatic, so quotable, so happy in his power to startle and sting the mind with the sudden surprise of beauty and of truth. His fertility of thought is matched by an exceeding aptness of imagery, as of one who thinks in pictures and talks in lyrics. His illustrations are both illuminative and instructive, as in a passage in his sermon on "Life's Criminal Agnosticism"—a title too harsh for the setting of the text—which tells what many have felt:

Do you read John Burroughs? You ought to. He likes dirt. He says dirt is good enough to eat in the spring. All told, as nature writers go, I think John Burroughs the best of all the sweet chorus. I have all his books except the one on Whitman. I have asked to be excused on that for a time. But do you read Burroughs' books? What is the lack of them? I will tell you. He has missed the Gardener. Burroughs is apparently an agnostic. I have gone through all his books, seen him walk on his dirt, gone down among the water lilies with him, stopped on the Hudson banks with him, heard the water brooks bubbling strangely intelligible speech with him, have been all wheres with him, but never saw a hint about the Gardener. If he only once had looked into the Gardener's face and said, "I bless thee, Gardener, that the garden is so sweet," Burroughs would have had no fellow in the earth as an interpreter of the out-of-doors. But in the garden he has missed the Gardener. We must not miss the Gardener. Is he at home? I call you to mark that you are out in God's flower garden, all a-bloom and all a-perfume, and all a-rapture of green. Do not miss the Gardener.[1]

In all the preaching of Bishop Quayle, at least in his later period—over it, through it—there is the breath and beauty of the out-of-doors; singing birds, growing flowers, drifting seas, and rustling woods, and the wandering

[1] *The Dynamite of God.*

brotherhood of the winds. No preacher of our
out-door age—not one—approaches him in his
love of nature and his vision of its meaning to
the spiritual life of man. He is a radiant
prophet of the everywhereness of God, a
"priest to us all of the wonder and bloom of
the world." As a naturalist, and still more as a
poet, he walks the earth with reverent, happy
feet, revealing to men the beauty at their doors,
no less than on far away hills, chanting the
eternal loveliness of earth and sky. He reads
God's Calendar so lovingly that if he were
to fall asleep and wake up, like Rip Van Win-
kle, he would know the time of year by the
flowers in bloom and the notes of bird-song in
the woodland. He knows the sea and its moods,
the far-stretching mystery of the prairies; the
mountains, the desert, the haunts of the birds
and the dells where the violets hide. All sea-
sons are his, summer with its splendour, and the
winter days when the north wind tumbles out
of his bed and goes romping over the hills,
sending the clouds scudding, and building the
snow into every form of frolic architecture.
To him trees are a means of grace, the fragrance of a rose is like a kiss of God, and the

sunlight falling on flowing waters is like the memory of one much loved and long dead. Like his Master, who taught out-of-doors, all nature is an infinite parable of God and he pours out his heart in poems of prayer and praise, reflection blooming into rapture and theology into song.

Joined with his love of nature is a lyric love of humanity, not unlike that of Browning, so genuine and joyous that all men feel the glow of it. Nothing human is alien to his insight and interest. He has an essay on "The Preacher as an Appreciator," and he is a model of his own precept. He knows "The Fine Art of Loving Folks"—all kinds and conditions of folk—and his worship of little children just stops short of idolatry. No wonder his book on *The Pastor-Preacher*—note the order of the words—is one of the richest of its kind, made so by his abounding humanity, no less than by his knowledge and experience of "preacher-craft." No one can talk to preachers as he can, unless it be Dr. Jefferson, and Quayle is more of a poet, more of a mystic. It would be hard to name anyone else who could have written the chapter on "The Preacher a

Mystic," in which we see that window in his
heart open toward the City of God, through
which falls a "light that never was on sea or
land." Seldom has genius been more com-
municative. The very informality of the book
is half its charm, dealing, as it does, both with
the trivialities and the sublimities of our holy
art. Never was there a more responsive listener or a more gentle-hearted critic. From
Spurgeon he derived little, Brooks he knows
only by report, but his tribute to Beecher is
memorable:

Since the apostolic days preaching, as
preaching, has never soared so high as in
Henry Ward Beecher. There were in him an
exhaustiveness and an exuberance, an insight
deep as the soul, a power to turn a light like
sunlight for strength on the sore weaknesses of
humanity, a bewilderment of approach to the
heart to tempt it from itself to God that I find
nowhere else; and it has been my privilege to
be a wide reader of the sermonic literature of
the world. Compared to him, Berry, the English preacher, whom Beecher thought most apt
to be his successor in the Plymouth pulpit, was
an instrument of a couple of strings matched
with Beecher's harp of gold. Phillips Brooks
cannot in any just sense be put alongside him;
and Simpson in his genius was essentially ex-

temporaneous and insular. Beecher was per-
petual, like the eternal springs. In Robertson
of Brighton are some symptoms of Beecher,
but they are cameo not building stone resem-
blances. Beecher was the past master of our
preaching art. Storrs and Beecher were con-
temporaries in the same city. Storrs was a
field of cloth of gold. Gorgeous he was, and
a man of might. But you cannot get from the
thought of effort in him and in his effects. In
Beecher is no sense of effort, any more than in
a sea bird keeping pace with a rushing ship. In
him are effortless music and might of a vast
power of reserve. This estimate of Beecher
may be right or wrong. I give it as my estimate of him. He has no successor, as Samson
had no son.

Some of us love Bishop Quayle best in his
little books of prayer, and we find *The Climb
to God* less to our need than *The Throne of
Grace*. They are years apart, and life has
taught him much betimes. The last named
rosary is deeper and more revealing, a kind of
diary of the soul written for God to read, like
the Confessions of Augustine. What music
and touch of deep truth, what unveiling of the
moods of the heart and its hunger for a more
than mortal fellowship. A deep and grateful
joy in God is joined with an eager, incessant

quest for more of God. On one page is a sinner abject at the mercy seat; on another he is a poet dropping roses at the feet of the Master. Half the time he is out of doors, rejoicing in "the beauty of the Lord our God," which is ever upon us in the wonder of his works. When we read "A Preacher's Prayer," we know him to be a kinsman, "proficient only in incompetency," as he is dazzled by the richness of the good news he is sent to tell. "Thy mandate is on my heart and on my lips. By thy command I am evangelist. Eternity is part of my parish. God help me." In prayer, in poem, in sermon the note of his genius is beauty; its depth is the depth that goes with beauty. It is as a great artist that he thinks of God, of Christ and of the life of man. In him the poet is supreme:

A man of sorrows He, and guest of grief,
  Who walked in quiet on life's humble ways
  And suffered all the slurs and dull dismays
Which crush on mighty souls. His days were
      brief—
A sudden splendour cleft with storm. Belief
  On Him grew dim, though great hearts
      walked through haze
  Of doubt and fogs of death with shouts of
      praise,

And knew Him glorious and acclaimed Him
    Chief.
And now He stands strange, uncompanied,
    vast,
Tall as all solemn, purpling mountains are—
Stands, while majestic, crumbling centuries
    waste.
The moaning travail of His soul is past.
He hath throned Love and wrought redemption
    far;
And who believeth on Him shall not haste.

XIII: George W. Truett

Three scenes are linked in my mind as I think of the career of Dr. Truett, whose ministry is one of the most remarkable in the history of the modern church. Taken together they show how God made a mighty preacher, endowed and trained him for his task, and set him in a place of influence and power. He is a truly great preacher, as much for the depth, simplicity and intensity of his faith as for the size, poise, and incommunicable charm of his personality. No man among us has more of what Joseph Parker called "the tone of great preaching," which might be the solicitude of a mother, the passion of a father, and the wooing note of a lover all in one. "Men are guided by type, not by argument," said Bagehot; "it is the life of teachers that is catching, not their tenets"; and that is supremely true of Dr. Truett, whose character fulfills the words of Amiel who said, "to be religious is to personify and embody the Eternal."

The first scene is from a biographical sketch of Dr. Truett, all too brief, which shows us the boy from the Blue Ridge Mountains at a meeting of the Baptists of Georgia, in the old courthouse at Marietta, in 1889. He was there to plead the cause of the youth of the mountains, as precious as gold for the miner's pick and fit to adorn the crown of a king. Tall, pale, shy, vastly embarrassed in the focus of so many eyes, the youth was forced into the aisle and led to the "prisoner's dock." There he told his story, forgetting himself—as he always does—and remembering only youth denied an opportunity of access to its rightful inheritance of knowledge. It was a simple story, but epic in its pathos of quiet recital of the passions, hopes, and longings of an unsung heroism. It grew more poignant with each word, until every heart was broken and yet athrill, moved alike by the merit of the plea and by the tones of a voice which carries the burden of tears which seems ever laid upon it. It was no pitiful plea of poverty—who ever heard that from a southern mountaineer?—but the cry of a youth in behalf of youth, the strong persuasion of a just matter, the logic of one who was resolved to let his own lack of opportunity plead for others. Suffice it to say that the young man of twenty-two went back to his mountain home taking new hope and joy with him.

Thence, after a time, the path of the young man led westward to Texas, where his parents had moved ahead of him. Within a few years he had saved a college from financial despair, had endowed it, had been graduated from it, and was elected to its presidency. Happily, and wisely, he did not accept the honour, keeping to the path marked out for his soul by One who made him to be a preacher. The triumphs of Dr. Truett—"plain, mountain-hearted, love-torn George Truett," in the words of one of his friends—read like a legend, as year by year he moved forward, divinely led while humbly following, to a place of command among his brethren. The man who wooed cowboys to their knees won cities also, until, in 1897, he came to the pulpit of the First Baptist Church of Dallas, a noble church destined to grow under his leadership to be one of the mighty forces of the nation, both in numbers and in spiritual fruitfulness. There, as pastor, teacher and evangelist, his genius has shone for more

than twenty years, where his name is a house-
hold word, and his fame is like a fragrance
throughout the nation.

The second scene was two years later, in
Louisville, at a meeting of the Baptist convention of the south in 1899, when Dr. Truett was
the preacher. It was a great occasion, and
there was a great orator to match it. The picture is vivid in my memory—the finely wrought
sermon, the burning earnestness of the preacher
—but no words of mine can describe a voice
which has in it an echo of that infinite pain
that throbs forever in the human heart; the
voice of one who knows that humanity is deeply
wounded, and that only Christ can heal it. The
sermon was entitled "The Subject and Object
of the Gospel," and was valuable not only for
its exposition of the theme but as a revelation
of the ideals of the preacher. He magnified his
office, and there were passages of stinging rebuke of clap-trap methods which degrade the
pulpit. "All sensationalism in the pulpit is
worse than sawdust," he said; it smacks of the
street and is a burning shame upon the Christian ministry. The following passage from the

sermon gives one clue to the secret of a
preacher who knows whereof he speaks, and in
whom the Christ-motif is supreme:

Nothing can take the place of the Christian
ministry. The progress of civilisation, the
making of many books, the increase of schools
and learning, the marvelous triumphs of the
press—mighty as are all of these agencies—
they can never supersede the divinely sent
preacher. . . . In the great crises of the past,
matchless has been the influence wielded by
God's prophets and preachers. When all other
voices have failed, they have rallied the waver-
ing people to the standards of truth and righteousness. It was the golden-mouthed Chry-
sostom who became the oracle of the hour in
the days when Antioch was smitten with terror.
It was the flaming Augustine who rallied his
fellow countrymen from despair and breathed
into their lives new hope and purpose, when imperial Rome lay bleeding and trampled beneath
the heel of an invading oppressor. It was the
plain, yet invincible Luther, who, when reeking
corruption reigned in the papal court and
spread its blight over all Europe, spoke forth
words that echoed as the thunder and were
piercing as the lightning, stirring a revolution
that thrilled all Christendom and marking a
new epoch in the civilisation of the world. As
in the past so shall it be in the future, that God's
foremost instrument is his preacher, in both

the civilisation and the evangelisation of the world.

There was an element in Paul's preaching that must needs be in all effective preaching. It was his tone of authority. He believed his message with all his heart, and as God's ambassador he delivered it without quailing, for one moment, under any fire. There is untold power in him who knows his mission is a thing of God's own willing, and that he cannot fail, though doubts may shroud in cloud the transient hour. It is conviction that convinces. The last place on earth for stammering and indefiniteness is the pulpit. Christ's ambassador is to proclaim his Master's message rather than to defend it. He is a witness rather than an advocate. Christianity is nothing if it is not sublimely positive. It is not a conundrum to be guessed at, or a theory to be speculated upon, but it is a divine revelation which is to be implicitly accepted and followed with the deepest heart-throb of our lives. To be continually on the defensive is contrary to the very genius and purpose of the gospel. The gospel faithfully preached is its own best defence.

The third scene was in Washington, in May, 1920, where the hosts of southern Baptists had assembled for their great convention—perhaps the greatest religious assembly in the world.

As the convention was held in the national
capital it was decided that there should be an
address setting forth the Baptist position with
regard to the relation of church and state; and
Dr. Truett was selected to deliver the address.
He stood on the front steps of the capitol building, looking toward the White House, and the
audience, numbering many thousands, filled the
open space.   Not for twenty years had I seen
Dr. Truett, and time had powdered his hair;
but the wonderful voice, with its haunting keys
and cadences, was the same.   The address was
entitled "Baptists and Religious Liberty," and
it was as much a sermon as an oration, review-
ing the long struggle for the freedom of faith,
and the part which Baptist heroes had in fighting the battle.   If it celebrated liberty, it was
also a plea for what Burke called "a manly,
moral, regulated liberty"; and it laid emphasis
upon the obligations which all true liberty im-
poses, lest it be used "for an occasion of the
flesh."   But liberty is not all.   Even if education be added to liberty it is not enough, for
"a democracy needs more than intelligence—it
needs Christ"; and the address closed with a
demand for evangelisation nation-wide, world-

wide, and ceaseless. For more than an hour the orator held the vast audience enthralled, and he sent us away with a solemn and overwhelming sense of the crisis of the modern world and its challenge to the Christian faith.

Someone said of Spurgeon that his theology, by itself, was abhorrent, but that it was never by itself. It was mixed with the stuff of the man, dipped and dyed in all the hues of his life, touched with spiritual genius and transfigured by a glorified common sense. In the same way, to many of us the theology of Dr. Truett would seem archaic, if not untenable, if we stopped to remember it. What we remember is not his theory but his experience, and we share and rejoice in the grand orthodoxy of the heart which makes his preaching so vital and compelling. Like the rest of us, when he argues he is weak; when he tells of the love of God and the saviourhood of Christ, he is irresistible. According to Aristotle—whose book on Rhetoric every preacher should study, if only to learn that rhetoric is not mere cookery, as Plato said in contempt—the office of the orator is persuasion, for which three qualities are necessary: prudence, moral excellence, and the good of the hearers at heart. No one fulfills these conditions more perfectly than Dr. Truett, whose character lights up like an altar lamp the teaching of his words. More than an evangelist, he is an evangel. As a rough man put it, unconsciously paying a high tribute, "He is a man who means it without trying to." His sincerity is not simply transparent, it is luminous. Men know that he loves them—they feel it—and that his one wish is to win them to Christ, and that to that end he spends his power without thought of himself. One of his friends has tried to describe his secret:

What is it that constitutes the acknowledged power of his preaching? In one answer all opinions meet. It is something in the man himself—the man behind the sermon, the incarnation of truthfulness in the messenger. Many sermons will yield to analysis the secret of their charm. Though many of the sermons of Truett have been reported in full, he belongs to that class of preachers who convince us that preaching is in the highest sense an incarnation, something more than a report of the truth, something more than the proclamation of the gospel. Whitfield could so speak the most commonplace words as to send chills through his audience. Truett has much of this power to communicate to men his soul on the most ordinary vehicles of thought and language. His words take on his spiritual quality as the dull black wire takes on the electric current.

Electricity, however, is scarcely a fortunate figure. He is least of all of the spectacular type. There is nothing angular or irregular in him. He has none of the personality run to seed—individualism on a pious spree. The strongest personalities are not eccentric. Eccentricity is unnecessary to such men. They have specific gravity beyond the need of peculiar advertisement. Too much of what men call personality in the pulpit, in the view that preaching is an incarnation, must hinder rather than help the gospel purpose. Is it possible that evangelism, which, reduced to the terms of psychology, is egotism, can be the appointed power of God unto salvation? The power of George Truett, as a preacher, can have no such explanation.

The phrase most often employed to explain Truett is "heart-power." Translated into visible, audible fact, it is this: A man of substantial flesh, enough to be a man of like passions with other men; an open Saxon face—a serious, some say a sad face; a voice set in a key of pathos; an impression of unfeigned sympathy, as of a man who has suffered, and whose pain, whatever it be, has become lost in a larger pain, through exchange of all personal life sorrows for the great human sorrow every-

where. In declining the presidency of Baylor
University he said simply in explanation: "I
have sought and found the shepherd's heart."
Perhaps there lies the hiding of his power.
Many have quoted the great avowal which
Frederic Myers puts into the mouth of Paul
the Apostle, but none whom I know can appropriate it more truly than Truett, when he
stands before a congregation of his fellow men
to preach the gospel that saves:

"Oft when the word is on me to deliver,
    Lifts the illusion and truth lies bare,
Desert or throng, the city or the river
    Melts in a lucid paradise of air.

"Only like souls I see the folk thereunder
    Bound who should conquer, slaves who
        should be kings;
Hearing their one hope with an empty wonder,
    Sadly content in a show of things.

"Then with a rush the intolerable craving
    Shivers throughout me like a trumpet call.
Oh, to save these, to perish for their saving,
    Die for their life, be offered for them all."

When all due allowance is made for the
beautiful exaggeration of friendship in this
tribute, these words do help us to know the
power of a preacher whose passion for human

souls is a consuming fire, and whose ministry
is attuned to the mighty music of redemption.
The latest volume of sermon by Dr. Truett is
by far the best, not only as a revelation of
deeper experience and riper powers, but because it preserves the whole of each service and
thus reproduces, as far as can be done in print,
the atmosphere of his personality. The com-
ments on the lessons, the prayers, the exhorta-
tions, the glowing appeals, all are reported in
full, erasing only such errors as are inevitably
due to rapid speaking and reporting. It is entitled *A Quest for Souls*—a title selected by
another, but exactly descriptive of the life-
passion of the preacher—and as an example
of evangelistic preaching at its highest it has
no volume to surpass it. As in his former
volume, *We Would See Jesus,* his homiletic
method is utterly simple and straightforward,
with no clever devices, no suggestion of sensation, nothing to deflect attention from the message. It is as free from the artificial and the
meretricious as the preacher himself is free
from the blandishments of flattery, wealth, or
fame. It is rich in illustration, drawn from
life, from history, from biography, from his

own wide observation, and especially from his
varied experience as a confidant of storm-vexed
human souls; but the illustration never once
gets in the way of the truth. Of the prayers
one hesitates to speak—they are so tender, so
direct, so aglow with insight and sympathy, so
intimate without being familiar, so haunting in
pathos yet so victorious in faith; as of one who
knows how to climb right up onto the knees of
God and talk with the simplicity of a little child.
The total impression of the volume does not
leave one thinking of the preacher at all—he is
quite forgotten—but of the Master whose he
is and whom he reveals; and it is hard to know
how any human being resisted such a series of
appeals.

Truly he is a winsome preacher of the winsomeness of Christ; one could not imagine the
gospel message being stained on his lip by
acerbity or odium. Always positive, always
persuasive, Dr. Truett has none of the grim,
harsh dogmatism of Torrey, none of the incredible vituperation which has disfigured so
much popular revivalism. He is an evangelist
of the Loving-Heart, not of threats and thun-
ders, and even in his most earnest moods his

gentleness is palpable, his good will unfailing. His thought and language are of the simplest. He knows how to be picturesque and full of colour, and he need only be himself to be richly human, but he never speaks except for a verdict. Instead of coming religiously to every point he comes at once to the point of religion, as when he began a sermon with the question: "Does not that boy over there wish to be a Christian, and that older one, turning into manhood, and that young man himself there, and that young woman—do you not wish to be Christians?" It is his explicit and purposeful "preaching for conversions" that makes it worth while, and very much worth while, studying him. An adherent of the older conception of Christianity, he is by that much ahead of the times, and the glib young liberals, who imagine they are progressive, are far behind. For, unless we are winners of human souls, we are not messengers of him who came to seek and to save that which is lost.

A famous master of Trinity College said of Maurice, after hearing him preach a university sermon: "There is about that man a kind of divine feeling or possession." More and more

this divine feeling, this supernatural grace,
seems to me to be the great distinction and
charm of Dr. Truett as a preacher. Other men
are greater scholars and profounder thinkers,
and there may be others who have something
of his artless simplicity of moving eloquence—
Gipsy Smith has much of it—but in his character as a Christ-anointed evangelist I doubt if
Dr. Truett is surpassed by any man in our
generation. Edmund Burke said of Charles
Fox: "That man was made to be loved"; but
his remark is of far nobler application to
George Truett. He was made to be loved. Indeed, it may be truly said that he does his best
work through the exalted and wonderful love
which he unconsciously and inevitably draws
toward himself. People do not try, do not care
to analyse or define his power; they simply love
him as one altogether worthy of their homage
and affection. Here is a burden of confidence
and devotion to make a man tremble; and it
must be added that no man ever used an opportunity with higher seriousness or nobler
power. Back into the hearts of the people he
pours through their love a tide of holy manhood, seeking to lift them by their love into the

redeeming fellowship of the great Lover. One thanks God for every remembrance of such a man, whose ministry is a benediction to the world and a theme of thanksgiving in the whole church of God.

XIV: Edward L. Powell

When a sermon is remembered for twenty-five years, and the very tones of the preacher still echo in the heart, it argues an unusual man in the pulpit; and thereby hangs a bit of reminiscence. In 1896, while a theologue in the Baptist Seminary at Louisville, I went with a number of my fellow students to the old Fourth and Walnut Street Church to hear the pastor, whom we greatly admired. It so happened that Dr. Eaton was not in the pulpit that day and, somewhat disappointed, we held conclave as to what we should do. Just opposite stood a plain, square, flat-roofed church without a spire, its wide porch and massive columns looking more like a Greek temple than a Christian shrine. Being in a mood for adventure, we strolled across the street, climbed the great stone steps, and entered the First Christian Church, to see what might transpire.

Of course we were severe critics, as young men are apt to be—especially theologues, who fancy they are wise—and our attitude of mind was biased, no doubt, by sectarian prejudice. Anyway, as there was no time to go to another church of proper faith and order, we took the risk, little knowing what revelations awaited us. What that day may have meant to others of the group I do not know, but it was one of the great days of my life, because it meant the discovery of one of the noblest preachers of our generation; a man as brotherly in private as he was brilliant in the pulpit, whose influence has been not only stimulating but emancipating, at once an inspiration and a benediction. The old Greek temple has vanished, along with the Fourth and Walnut Street Church, both having been removed from the centre of the city, where they had stood for so many years, bearing witness, each with its own eloquence, to the reality of the Unseen in the midst of time.

The First Church was crowded to the doors, but a kindly usher found chairs and tucked us away in a far corner, just as the preacher entered the pulpit. Not one of us had ever seen the preacher before, having for the first time read his name as we entered the church—a fact which gives the measure of our abysmal igno-

rance. Across the years I can still see Dr.
Powell as he stood that day, in the prime and
glory of his power—his slight figure, his huge
head, his thin, light hair, his keen, searching
eyes—not a graceful man, his gestures angular
at times, his face aglow with unearthly light,
uttering his high message in words vivid, full
of grace, and surcharged with living fire. It
was a vision unforgettable. He conducted the
service less as a leader of worship than as a
leading worshipper—it was all so simple, so
reverent, so impressive. He read the Bible as
one who was himself a listener at the portals of
a book where "the sweet voice sounds and the
vision dwells. The prayer was direct, tender,
and far ranging in its sympathies, as of one
who remembered only the sublime object of his
office, to lift men out of the mire of sin, ma-
terialism, and the bewilderments of life into the
higher air of God. It besought the grace of
God in that moral self-legislation which each
man must enact and execute, if he is to verify
faith in character.

The sermon began quietly, all eyes fixed upon
the preacher, some eager, some tender, all interested. It had to do with the holiness of God,

taking as its text the vision of Isaiah in the temple, and surely no one ever forgot the terrifying vision of a universe ruled by an unholy God, where men sit by the poisoned springs of life, looking at polluted flowers, and lifting up hands to abominable hills. Man can endure an indifferent world. He does not lose heart when told that the flowers are heartless, and would as soon adorn a grave as a bridal altar. But a malignant universe is intolerable. Not only the value but the very existence of the soul is in jeopardy, and all our dear human world is cast into shadow, "pent up in the kingdom of pity and death." It made the very soul shudder, and there are times when a shudder is an argument. Then followed, by contrast, a picture of a lucid and wise order where righteousness reigns, where every mountain is an altar, and all the laws of life are God's ten thousand commandments: a picture appropriate to a Greek temple—the vision of a man who sees the holiness of beauty, no less than the beauty of holiness. He had not spoken two paragraphs before the spark caught, and the man, his theme, and his audience were alike transfigured. His slight figure seemed to tower aloft to the pro-

portions of a giant; his voice vibrated with
moral electricity; his burning words became a
torrent, yet all was held in bound by a firm,
directing hand. It was a revelation of "truth
through personality," as Phillips Brooks defined
preaching; what George MacDonald called
"the rare speech of a man to his fellows
whereby they know that in his innermost heart
he is a believer."

No skill of oratory could have produced that
sermon; it came from no such art. It came
from something beyond creeds, something far
beyond differences of theology and methods of
worship. It was that old, haunting, pathetic,
subduing, thrilling voice heard in all ages of the
church, amidst the splendours of mediæval superstition, as in the fiery appeal of modern revivalism. Older than Christianity itself, it is
more vivid than music and more eloquent than
architecture, and its spell is as mysterious as
the wind in the trees. Such words have stirred
the souls of men in every age, winning restless,
wayward spirits by their divine passion, and
turning bloodshed and rapine into righteous
crusades. Whether spoken on bare hillsides
beneath a crucifix, or in a plain white country

meeting house, such words can never lose their power while human nature is the same. This quality of spirituality, so rare in men of great powers, inspires a kind of awe. Men bow to it, as a field of grain bows at the breath of the wind, feel themselves in the presence of the Unseen, and are touched, if only for a moment, by a sense of wonder and regret.

There is no need to say that I became a regular attendant at the old First Church, much to the scandal of my seminary, where I was reckoned a black sheep in the flock. It seemed to me that the sermon of that day was the achievement of a lifetime; but so far from being exceptional, I learned that it was typical of a preacher who always invested the facts of Christian faith with commanding certainty and practical urgency. As often as I heard Dr. Powell, he always seemed able instantly to realise that release of personality—what the old time Methodists called "liberty"—without which preaching is the hardest work ever undertaken by mortal man; harder than making brick without straw. Tales are told of his failures—as in Richmond one night when his sermon went from him entirely—but never

once have I heard him when he did not trans-
mute his thoughts into fire and light to kindle
and illumine, and it was always light without
smoke. Less scholarly than Broadus, less
rhetorical than Gunsaulus—two of his peers
now fallen asleep—he is more virile than
Jowett, having none of that flowery emptiness
which is the besetting sin of the "poet-
preacher." Indeed, he knows nothing of the
dainty, prettified, pietistic gospel so dear to the
dilettante, and no doubt that is why he appeals
so strongly to strong men, uniting a vivid faith
with a vital, winsome, and enthusiastic manhood. Besides, judged by any test, Dr. Powell
is one of the great orators of his day, though
not the equal of his uncle, Dr. Robert C. Cave
—the most perfect orator I have ever heard
speak, alike in matter and in manner.

One has only to turn to a volume of his sermons—all too rare, alas—such as *The Victory of Faith,* to know the quality of Dr.
Powell and his ministry. They are the words
of a man familiar with the most perfect fruits
of culture and sensitive in high degree to the
charms of literary form. Not merely in palpable allusion, but in the choice phrase, the

brilliant epigram, the modulations of his sentences, and a most chaste verbal reserve, is to be discerned the master of speech. As sacred compositions they captivate as much by their beauty as by their forthrightness of insight and appeal. They are logical without any display of argument, and poetical without any sacrifice of directness and sincerity. Reason is appealed to all along, but the language of the appeal comes up all blossoming and fragrant with the heart. No one can fail to recognise their catholicity of spirit, their gracious aim, and their helpfulness to mind that recoil from the formal and arbitrary in religion. Only the commanding vitalities of Christianity and its heroic enterprise engage his heart and inspire his ministry. He cares nothing for hair splitting dogmas, but for those heavenly truths which overarch all creeds, and that life of the spirit, "mystical in its roots and practical in its fruits," which underlies all sects. As we may read, turning the pages swiftly:

What is the preacher's world? Answer may be made that he is the messenger of religion; as Ralph Connor would say, he is the "sky pilot." But when we begin to think of what religion means—that it has to do with all life and therefore with all things, that it claims all provinces of thought and activity for its territory—we begin to see that the preacher as a messenger of religion must be a many-sided individual, and must touch life in one way or another at almost every point. The religion of Jesus has to do with all men and all things, and with all of a man—body, soul, and spirit. And he who would proclaim that religion must be a man of the world in the best sense. The more he knows of life, the more effectively he can meet the requirements of human need.

. . . . .

Should a preacher enter politics? Not as a profession, but in the proclamation of righteousness he must necessarily have to do with the politician and with the affairs of state, even as in preaching honesty, purity, love, he is declaring principles that touch every business and avocation in life. The preacher cannot be sidetracked during the week or given to understand that his business belongs to Sunday and the church. Every day is his day of opportunity; every realm is his field of service and duty; all places, if they be entered in the spirit of his Master, furnish him with a pulpit. To the extent that preaching becomes a mere profession —having to do with certain things that can be labelled and classified, the preacher is provincial. In the words of Wesley, the preacher has the world for his parish. I do not know any man who requires a deeper, richer or fuller life for his work than does the preacher.

. . . . .

The imperialism of Jesus takes the whole life of man for its kingdom. His rule within the heart of man must manifest itself in every part of man's environment. He cannot govern the inner life apart from the outer. The whole frame-work of society is, therefore, involved in the imperial programme of Jesus. Poverty, vice and crime are inconsistent with the present social condition of our great cities. The Bible, through and through, insists upon the redemption of the bodies of men, as well as their souls, and of the whole frame-work of human society. And so the regency of Christ contemplates the bringing of our homes, our politics, our trade— all the means, agencies and things with which we are connected—under the sway of Jesus.

. . . . .

Consider the sweeter, nobler, conceptions of religion which are ours today. As life takes colour from Christianity it is ennobled. Today life is happier, stronger, because of the things we have left behind. The church is journeying away from the falsities of mediævalism, but carries forward the sweetness and light of Jesus. Gone forever the hideous dogmas that tortured our fathers. Gone the dogmas which confused Satan with God. The church is exchanging the worship of the past for the heritage of the present, the old philosophies for

the new living Christ. We know more, and
therefore we love more. The certificate of
Christianity is something more than proved
propositions. It is a helpful life. There has
come a new conscience which makes it impossible for men to be content to have, while their
brothers have not. The physical misery of the
world's disinherited is becoming the spiritual
misery of the world's elect.

Happy is the city which has sent to it an
authentic messenger of great truths; one of
those elect spirits to whom religious cares and
interests are what secular cares and interests
are to other men. For thirty years Dr. Powell
has laboured in Louisville, at the gateway of
the South—himself a Virginian gentleman of
the old school—taking not only a city but a com-
monwealth for his parish, with a public influence only equalled by his indefatigable industry
as a pastor. Resisting all temptations to leave
Louisville, he added year to year, decade to
decade, with a continuity and cumulative mo-
mentum of influence, giving him a command
of the higher life of a city such as few men
have ever attained. Through all the years he
has played well his part in practical affairs, but
his life is not there. The growth of the king-

dom of grace is his prosperity, the application of Christian ideas to life is his supreme concern. Less a reformer than a former of the ideals and conscience of a great community, all through his ministry he has fearlessly dealt with public issues, and always from a Christian point of view. Never a pulpit scold, never falling into a pessimistic or denunciatory tone—like the Queen in *Alice in Wonderland,* who said there was jam yesterday, and there will be jam tomorrow, but there is no jam today—by the weight of his character, by the wisdom of his practical suggestion, no less than by the power of his passionate eloquence, he has wrought mightily as a preacher and leader of righteousness.

There was a time, years ago, when Kentucky was torn by a bitter political feud, becoming almost an armed camp, and the governor-elect was shot dead in the capital city. With triumphant tact, with unfaltering courage, Dr. Powell made it an opportunity for some of the greatest preaching of his life, rebuking iniquity, and pleading for the fundamental moralities of private and public life. Later, when the chief executive of the state was a fugitive in

an adjoining state, it was the pulpit of the old
First Church that spoke in behalf of forgive-
ness, making plea equally for Christian common sense and public decency. It was a difficult
—nay, a disgraceful—time, but Dr. Powell
dealt with it in a manner forever memorable,
revealing the political function of religion and
the strategy of Christian leadership. Fortunately some of the sermons, addresses, and
articles of that period were gathered into a
little book, entitled *Savonarola, and Other
Addresses on Civic Righteousness,* in which
we may read to this day the heartache of a
patriot and the testimony of a prophet. His
ringing call to "Sleeping Citizenship," his fine
appeal to "Public Men and Morals," his thrilling commentary on the Battle Hymn of the
Republic—itself a prose-poem of no mean
order—and his noble interpretation of "The
Divine Presence in Political History," the last
two evoked by the Spanish-American war—
show us how a Christian can be a patriot, and
a patriot a Christian. In the same way, during
the Great War, when his body was frail and
his heart wrung with agony, his pulpit was an
altar alike of Christian faith and patriotic fire.

For some of us Louisville is a city of many memories, not only of days that come not back, but of great scholars and dear teachers whose influence abides, and of fellowships which time cannot destroy. It is the city of Henry Watterson, last and greatest of the editors of the old days of chivalrous and brilliant journalism; the golden voice of the south and a national character. It is the city of Mary Anderson, and *Mrs. Wiggs of the Cabbage Patch;* of Madison Cawein, a lyric poet whose song was heard and loved in England, even before it won its way at home. It has ever been a city of great preachers, like Broadus, Boyce, Hemphill, Hamilton, Pickard, Dudley, Eaton, and Rabbi Adolph Moses, a stately, grave, and noble teacher. Many have fallen asleep but Powell remains, the peer and comrade of a goodly company, the best beloved and—now that Watterson has vanished—the most famous citizen of his city.

XV: Frank W. Gunsaulus

In Memoriam

As I sit down to write in appreciation of the genius of Dr. Gunsaulus as a preacher, the news tells me that he has gone to his crowning. It is heavy tidings, and like thousands of young men all over the land, to whom he was as much father as friend, I am lonely and forlorn. It seems impossible to realise that his abounding personality, his incandescent vitality, his pure and winsome manhood are now only a memory, and that we are never to hear that golden voice again on earth. The words from the old Hebrew centuries flash into my mind: "My father! My father! The chariots of Israel and the horsemen thereof!" Alas, my appraisal becomes a memorial, and I can make no reader of mine understand with me, remembering almost twenty years of unbroken friendship, how a gracious presence—majestic, magnetic, commanding, enchanting—stands yet vividly before me, refusing to say farewell.

No doubt there will be a biography of Dr. Gunsaulus, but one cannot be sure of it. Chicago is neglectful of its great personalities. Gentle, wise, meditative David Swing had to wait for more than twenty years—until it was almost too late—and even now there is no life-story of Dr. Harper who, alike in character and achievement, must be reckoned among the great Americans. A biography of Gunsaulus, if written, will show us a man of many manifestations, and it will tell a story more thrilling than any romance. Poet, artist, scholar, educator, author, orator, statesman, and, above all, a God-endowed preacher whose mysticism was at once the inspiration and illumination of his multifarious activity—it is a story of which America ought to be proud. He was the first citizen of his city, if not the most distinguished—the incarnation of its genius and the prophecy of its future. Uniting the fine, firm qualities of the Puritan with the glow, colour and tropical richness of Spain, he also joined the skyey vision of the poet with the practical acumen of a man of affairs. Words are the daughters of earth, deeds are the sons of God, and both were wedded in his life. Fortunately

I am to write of him only as a preacher, but even in that capacity one may well despair of describing a man whose personal and intellectual charm none could define and few resist.

Already the early eloquence of Gunsaulus is a legend of magic and mystery. Only recently a man related how he sat with a friend on the floor in the aisle of Plymouth Church, during the Columbian Exposition, and heard the pastor preach. It was the enchantment of pure genius, an oratory more vivid than music in which every gesture seemed an event. He read his text from Exodus 4:4, "And the Lord said unto Moses, Put forth thine hand, and take it by the tail. And he put forth his hand, and it became a rod in his hand." Both men wondered what could be made out of such a text, but they did not have long to wait. The appetites and passions of a man, like snakes, coil and wriggle at his feet until, at the command of God, he grasps them firmly. Then they become sceptres of sovereignty, wands of moral authority—forging passion into power. But no art can bring back the magic whereby the orator swept all before him, holding men as if their own soul spoke to them in his words, as he described the fight every man must wage with himself if he is to be a man. Standing back from the pulpit, brushing his long raven hair from his forehead, his eyes kindling with a dusty yet piercing light, "orb within orb," he swayed his audience as the wind sways the clouds. There was nothing artificial, no studied unnatural effect, but the fire and rapture of great eloquence dedicated to the service of the moral life. To this day, though twenty-seven years have come and gone, my friend can repeat not only the idea and outline of that sermon, but whole passages of its music.

As early as 1881—to go back for a time in my story—the young preacher saw, prophetically, that theology must be translated into sociology. When he came to Chicago, six years later, the Armour Mission lay ready to his hand, and he laid hold of it, lavishing upon it his love and labour. Some months later he preached a sermon in which he not only unburdened the passion of his heart for the young, but, as was equally characteristic, outlined a practical plan and remedy. At the conclusion of the sermon, Philip D. Armour came forward with a direct, searching question:

"Do you really believe in those ideas you have just expressed?" said the captain of industry.

"I certainly do," answered the preacher.

"Well, then, if you will give me five years of your time, I will furnish the money," was the reply; and that sermon became known as the two million dollar sermon.

Out of that sermon grew Armour Institute, the history and growth of which should make more than one chapter in the biography of the preacher. With that story I have not to do now, except to say that, while one does not see how Dr. Gunsaulus could have escaped the opportunity and burden of so prodigious an undertaking—and, manifestly, he did not desire to escape—it none the less divided the interests of his life, and diverted the full tide of his genius from the pulpit. Indeed, he was more than once ready—and actually tried—to resign the pulpit altogether and devote himself entirely to education, as he finally did two years ago. Yet there are fifty men who can conduct and develop a technical institute, for every one whom God has endowed with the rare and precious genius of a great preacher. A giant in strength, of fabulous mental and spiritual resource, he did the work of many men, adding labour to labour—the institute and the church being only two items in an incredible number of activities—though I have often wondered if it had not been better had he obeyed the example of St. Paul, "this one thing I do," in single-hearted devotion.

At any rate, Dr. Gunsaulus made his decision, did his work—and paid the price! The call of a great growing city, and the pathos of its spiritual need, lured him on. As if his church and the institute were not enough, he began a great downtown Sunday evening service in Central Music Hall, which was packed to the doors. At length the inevitable happened. The man of iron broke. Physical collapse—complete and shattering—befell him in 1897, and for six months he lay motionless on a bed of agony. No sermons came from the preacher then, no books; only a poem. That poem revealed his intrepid and unconquerable spirit:

I care not that the furnace fire of pain
  Laps round and round my life and burns alway;

I only care to know that not in vain
  The fierce heats touch me throughout night
    and day.

When he returned to Plymouth pulpit, a quivering sigh, not unmixed with horror, ran
through the congregation. A terrible thing
had happened. Valiantly he had wrestled with
the Angel of Pain in the twilight, and it had
left him lame and misshapen of frame. He had
been tall, agile, handsome as a Greek god, and
now he was doomed to go limping to the end.
One leg behaved like a dead thing. Later,
when Lorenz of Vienna tried with his deft
fingers to untie the knot, he said with grim
Teutonic humour, "Cheer up! There is no hope
for you." He did cheer up. For, in the fiery
furnace of pain Another had walked with him
betimes. New windows of insight had been
opened, new depths of experience fathomed,
and new and haunting stops of music had been
mastered!

It was on Sunday, November 30, 1902,
that I first heard Gunsaulus preach, and the
wonder of that day is still vivid in my heart.
Such a voice cannot be made in one generation!
Today its tones come back to me from behind

the hills, now soft as a flute, now melodious as
an orchestra, with never a note to jar. It was
as variable as the moods of the man, as just as
his character, as sweet as his spirit. It was
the Sunday after the death of Joseph Parker,
and the sermon was a vision of the Christian
ministry as illustrated in the life of the first
minister of the City Temple. They had been
friends—the preacher and his subject—and
some allowance had to be made for the beautiful bias of friendship in his estimate of Parker.
It was an extraordinary portrayal, as touch
after touch was added to the picture, until at
last Joseph Parker seemed to live again in the
pulpit of Central Church. As I had never seen
Parker, it was like a revelation to me, albeit
I could not follow him when at times he seemed
to place him above Beecher. From the notes
of that day I transcribe a passage, if only because the sermon was a revelation equally of
the subject and of the preacher, and because it
will help to make clear what, to me, at least,
was the greatest quality of Dr. Gunsaulus as a
preacher. Thus:

It is an awful risk God takes in creating a
David or a Robert Burns. But they justify it,

for they give a double significance to nature
and life. Such men recreate the external world
and its events into an internal order made
richer by the language they learn. David,
Burns, Augustine, with varying colours portray
to us the cost and the peril of letting loose a
great soul on the earth. Joseph Parker, by the
grace of God, made gigantic mistakes; but also,
by the grace of God, he avoided many pitfalls
which such a genius digs for a man. I regard
him as a wonderfully endowed and restrained
man. He could never have been a little sinner;
he was not a little saint. The stone-mason's
boy has not opened unto us the Scriptures, and
Gladstone and the kitchen-maid, Sir Henry
Irving and the bootblack, have not listened to
be pleased for so many years, without demon-
strating that the mark of such a nature is capacity for pain.

A great man and a great theme—Joseph
Parker with the Scriptures of God and man—
how marvellously they re-enforce and illustrate
each other! He had so meditated upon the
Scriptures and lived with kings, prophets,
psalmists and captain of the Bible that he became a part of them and they of him. When
he preached upon David, it was no small man
attempting to measure the girth of the poet-
king. Parker was David at the time. One
instant it was the boy looking into the heights
of manhood as he talked with Samuel; the next,
it was the man looking down from physical

safety and moral insecurity from his palace into the defenseless home of Uriah. When he preached on Isaiah, one saw how unobstructedly the prophet-statesman of Israel moved in the City Temple pulpit. Exegesis like this is a matter of complete personality; it is not a matter of learning Greek or skill in analysis. The legend of his eloquence will be told by many generations!

Here is an example of the style of Dr. Gunsaulus—at times so curiously involved and lacking in lucidity, and often so luxuriant as to bewilder—but the significant thing is that he seized upon that in Joseph Parker most akin to himself, his power of dramatic characterisation. In this art Gunsaulus himself was at his best, and in the use he made of it we have had no one like him in America; no one near him. Such an art—depending so much upon gesture, facial expression, and the dramatic personality of the preacher—loses three-fourths of its spell and wonder on the printed page. No printed sermon by Dr. Gunsaulus shows us more than half the man. Alas, much the same is true of every great preacher—his art dies with him, becoming a vacancy that is vacated with the passing of the generation to whom he minis-

tered—but it is doubly so with a preacher like
Gunsaulus. If only by some art we could re-
capture and perpetuate the magic spell of his
genius, that as little as possible may be lost of
the precious treasure of mankind!

Howbeit, all that one can do in such a sketch
as this is to indicate, in some measure, not what
Dr. Gunsaulus had in common with other
preachers, but the gift which was uniquely and
supremely own. And that, as I have said,
was his genius for dramatic characterisation.
Two of his sermons may serve as examples,
two of the greatest sermons I have ever heard,
and I doubt if anyone else could have preached
either one of them. One dealt with the Temptation of Jesus, and the vision of the Master,
worn, weary, weak from hunger and long vigil,
standing—a lone and quivering soul—face to
face with the subtle cunning of ultimate Evil,
feeling its fearful fascination, can never be forgotten! The other sermon—it has never been
printed, I believe—might have been entitled,
"Jesus at the Feet of his Disciples," and had to
do with the evening in the Upper Room when
the Master washed the feet of his Apostles.
"And He took a towel," was the text. "He

might have taken a star!" said the preacher, the better to show the august humility of the Servant in the House. Then he became an artist, reproducing not only the scene, but the atmosphere of the farewell meal. All at once he began to re-enact the scene, from the point of view of each disciple, as the Master approached him with basin and towel. Only a man of painter-like sympathy and dramatic insight could have done it. A single false note would have ruined the scene, but there was no false note. Each disciple stood out distinctly—his character, his personality, his very soul—as if, by some magic, the man had been there in the pulpit. The preacher forgot himself—the congregation forgot the preacher—all were present again in the Upper Room long ago. One could have taken a photograph of Simon Peter, it was so real, so vivid. It was a solemn, almost terrifying moment when he came to Judas; strong men sobbed like children, torn equally between the horror of evil obsession and the awful mercy of the Master. Never again on this earth do I expect to hear such a sermon, now that the great artist-preacher has vanished!

Memories crowd upon me, among them a
radiant Easter service in the Auditorium Thea-
ter, every seat of which was filled with an
eager, expectant humanity. I entered the top
gallery just as the vast congregation bowed,
like a field of grain touched by a soft wind, and
the prayer began with these words: "O God,
in the far distances of Thy fatherhood we were
conceived in love; from Thy fatherhood we
have come we do not know how far." What
a sentence! I had journeyed two hundred
miles to the service, and that sentence was
worth the journey. After a hymn, the words
of which he himself had written, the preacher
began his sermon, taking for his text the
words: "If a man die shall he live again?"—
words that come wailing across perplexed and
anxious ages, pathetic, heroic, awful! For an
hour the preacher spoke out of a deep heart and
a clear mind, using every kind argument,
imagery and appeal,—hints, flashing phrases,
glowing apostrophes, intricate facts of science,
and radiant insights that just stopped short of
rhapsody. Men listened believing, or wanting
to believe, and the scene comes back to me today, now that the preacher has passed into the

life of which he spoke with passionate and persuasive eloquence. These words from the closing prayer echo in my heart: "O Lord, may we realise that Thou hast done Thy divinest for man in compelling him to cut the path and fathom the mystery of pain." [1]

There is no need to say that Dr. Gunsaulus was the orator, not the theologian, nor yet the man of letters—a man who ruled by his grace and charm of spirit, rather than by his originality and potency of thought—though his scholarship was thorough, and his books are rewarding, especially his historical novel, *The Monk and the Knight*. He was indeed almost the last of the old Gladstonian school of the elaborate and rounded period, using the full-

[1] Happily we now have a volume of *The Pulpit Prayers of Dr. Gunsaulus,* edited by his daughter, Helen, and dedicated to the great preacher "who, a year ago this Easter-time, entered completely into the life eternal which he illumined for his fellowmen during all the years of his ministry." The prayers, taken down verbatim during the services of Central Church, cover the period between 1913 and 1918, and are grouped as invocations, petitions, prayers in war-time, and on special occasions. The little book brings back the echo of a voice now hushed on earth, but which still lives in the hearts of a vast company to whom it spoke, as from the sky, words of comfort and command. Some of us can almost see the characteristic gesture—the towering figure, the noble head, the arms outstretched to embrace—as if the preacher sought to gather his congregation to his heart, and on the wings of his prayer lift them into the higher air of God, and detain them there for cleansing and consecration.

throated Latin family of words. In early days
his style—warm, exuberant, chromatic—often
had all the lurid tropic colouring of Hugo, re-
splendent and sometimes grandiose; but in later
years it had softened and chastened its hues.
More often, toward the end, he struck a calmer
key in which, with hardly a movement of the
body, with the slightest employ of any dramatic suggestion, he held his hearers by the
depth of his insight, the richness of his experience of things immortal, and the nameless
grace of his spirit. Some of us thought his
lecture on "The Heroism of Scholarship" far
more admirable than his "Gladstone" or his
"Savonarola." He was not always triumphant,
and if his successes were noble and moving, his
failures were equally gorgeous—like that awful
day in the City Temple when he took for his
theme the death of Florence Nightingale, and
the sermon simply did not come off. Even at
his worst he was never commonplace, never
cheap, and the contagious quality of his personality—by its generosity, its amplitude, its
winsomeness—redeemed many an ill-starred
effort.

Alas, how inadequate is my analysis and estimate of a man so radiant and radiating, so brotherly withal and lovable; the Friar Gonsol of Eugene Field's rare and quizzical book, *The Temptation of Friar Gonsol.* To know him was to become, if not actually generous, like him, at least indisposed—partly indeed unable —to judge him calmly, much less critically. He was enchanting in the warmth of his fellowship, his boyish joy in life, the vividness of his enthusiasm, and the unfeigned simplicity of his modesty. Never will his young brethren forget his gay heart, his glittering mind, his generosity of appreciation, his self-giving so open-hearted and open-handed, his verve, dash and gentleness—what times we talked the hours away. He had a talent for living and a genius for friendship. But the deepest thing in him —the still centre of his busy, fruitful life—was his poet-soul, and its experience of God in Christ. Before me lie letters telling, man to man, his faith in Jesus in words as simple as the prayer of a child—letters so lovely that they make the heart ache. Anyone who knew him, and the rising and falling moods out of which his poems were born, can trace his real biography in his songs. They disclose a tender, wistful, beauty-loving spirit, sensitive to all Divine persuasions, uniting a large and living culture with a heroic faith; a faith not held without struggle in a world pent up in "the kingdoms of pity and death," where life is woven of beauty, mystery, and sorrow. His own words return to tell us whither he has gone:

> From moonlight, night and wonder,
>   He stepped to sunlight yonder—
>   The poet's paradise.
>
> His lyre with string unbroken,
>   Will ring like music spoken,
>   And tremble toward God's day.

THE END